BEGINNING AT THE BEGINNING

Sermons from the Book of Genesis

Beginning at the Beginning

Sermons from the Book of Genesis

Graham Harrison

BRYNTIRION PRESS

Scripture quotations, unless otherwise indicated, are from
the Authorised (King James) Version.

Cover design: Phil Boorman

Published by Bryntirion Press
Bryntirion, Bridgend CF31 4DX, Wales, UK
Printed by WBC Book Manufacturers, Bridgend

For
the congregation of Emmanuel Chapel
who first heard these sermons and who
continue to listen receptively to
the preached word.

Contents

Preface

Genesis is where it all began, and the history the book contains sets the scene for the unfolding message of the Bible. Thus its importance as the starting point of revelation cannot be overestimated; which makes its relegation by so many would-be expositors to the fictitious realm of myth and fable the more tragic.

These evangelistic sermons which were preached in Emmanuel Chapel, Newport, on Sunday evenings from September to November 1987 are printed substantially as they were delivered, with the omission of some passing contemporary allusions. A generation that does not know who it is, where it has come from, or where it is going, needs to listen to what God is still telling it through this ancient but ever relevant narrative. I pray that the Lord will be pleased to use these sermons to that end.

Chapter One
How it all went wrong

*And the Lord God said, Behold, the man is
become as one of us, to know good and evil: and now,
lest he put forth his hand, and take also of the tree of life,
and eat, and live for ever: therefore the Lord God sent
him forth from the garden of Eden, to till the ground
from whence he was taken. So he drove out the man; and
he placed at the east of the garden of Eden Cherubims,
and a flaming sword which turned every way, to
keep the way of the tree of life.*
(Genesis 3:22-24)

These verses come at the end of what in many ways is the saddest chapter in the whole of the Bible. It is the chapter that tells us of how man fell from a state of innocence and virtue into a state of alienation from God— rebellion against God, self-will, antagonism to God, a state in which he is placed under the judgment of God. I want to preach on this chapter because it is certainly to be numbered amongst the most important chapters in the Bible.

Now that may come as a surprise to some of you who may be in the habit of thinking, when you come to these early chapters of Scripture, that they are not very far removed from the realm of fairy stories. This is probably the sort of thing that you learned in school. It might even be the sort of thing that you have had put to you from pulpits, by men who ostensibly were preaching to you the Word of God. The suggestion has been that this is really in the realm of myth and fantasy; that if you ponder it, there may be one or two lessons that you can learn from it, but no right-thinking person in these days could ever be expected to take what happened in these chapters as something literally and historically true. Therefore, when I say that a chapter like this must be numbered amongst the most important chapters of Scripture, there is probably something in your heart which rejects what I am saying, something which silently says to me, in effect, that I really don't know what I am talking about, and that in expressing myself like that I am making a great miscalculation.

A key chapter

Why have I put it in this way? I have done so for this reason: you do not understand the rest of the Bible unless you come to terms with what is revealed to us here in Genesis chapter 3. More than that, you do not really understand the world as it is today, unless you have an understanding of what took place there in the Garden of Eden (how long ago I do not know) when our first parents rebelled against God. You have no explanation adequate to satisfy the thinking of anybody who faces issues as they really are, unless you are able to understand what God has caused to be recorded for us in this portion of his Word. Why is it, for example, that instead of the world getting better and better, it seems to get worse and worse? Why is it that whenever we turn on our news programmes, on the radio or television, we are confronted invariably by stories of tragedy and war, sexual lust and violence, some sort of injustice perpetrated by one man, or one group of men, against another? That is the sort of world that we live in.

Now why is it like that? Why is it that in a world in which, as some people would have us believe, human beings are evolving and rising to ever higher levels of attainment, people are not able to live in peace with one another? Why is it that they tell lies? Why is it that they lust after what belongs to somebody else—whether it is another man's wife, or another man's possessions, or another nation's country? Why is it that men don't grow up and really begin to act in a rational and sensible way? Why? The world hasn't an answer for that. The politicians do not have answers. The philosophers do not have answers. But the Bible has an answer—and the answer of the Bible begins here in this third chapter of the book of Genesis. It tells us clearly why the world is as it is, and how the world has come to be as it is.

Of course, it is not the beginning of the Bible! There are two chapters that come before this third chapter of Genesis, and you do not really understand this chapter unless you are familiar, in outline at least, with the earlier chapters. They tell us about a God who exists in splendid independence and isolation: a God who needs nobody, a God who needs nothing, a God who is entirely self-existent. And yet that God called into existence this earth, this universe in which we live. When he made the earth it was perfect, for it is impossible for a perfect God to make anything less than perfect. So in it there was no sin, no tendency to sin, nothing to spoil the handiwork of God. Thus we read at the end of the account of the Creation that God looked at all that he had made and saw that it was very good (Genesis 1:31). There was no flaw at all, nothing whatsoever to spoil what God had brought into being.

In the second chapter, we have a quite detailed account of how God created the first man and then his wife. We are told that he placed them in what is called the Garden of Eden—a place of beauty and perfection, where everything that man could need for his livelihood was round about him. God put him under probation. He gave him just one restriction. He could eat of every tree that was in the garden, except for one. There was a prohibition placed on the tree of the knowledge of good and evil. God warned him not to eat its fruit, 'for in the day that thou eatest thereof thou shalt surely die' (Genesis 2:17).

The second chapter gives us, in brief outline, a picture of man in the state of perfection, in fellowship and harmony with God, with nothing to come between him and the wife that God has given him, this woman called Eve. There is perfect harmony, perfect delight, peace and joy. Then you come to the third chapter, and immediately you sense that there is a change:

Now the serpent was more subtil than any beast of the field which the LORD God had made. And he said unto the woman, Yea, hath God said, Ye shall not eat of every tree of the garden? And the woman said unto the serpent, We may eat of the fruit of the trees of the garden: but of the fruit of the tree which is in the midst of the garden, God hath said, Ye shall not eat of it, neither shall ye touch it, lest ye die. And the serpent said unto the woman, Ye shall not surely die: for God doth know that in the day ye eat thereof, then your eyes shall be opened, and ye shall be as gods, knowing good and evil. And when the woman saw that the tree was good for food, and that it was pleasant to the eyes, and a tree to be desired to make one wise, she took of the fruit thereof, and did eat, and gave also unto her husband with her; and he did eat (Genesis 3:1-6).

From that moment, sin entered this world of perfection that God had made.

Historicity

If you ask me why I, or any other reasonably intelligent person, presume to believe that something like this really happened, I will tell you. It is because the Lord Jesus Christ believed that it happened. The Lord Jesus Christ asserted what we sometimes call the historicity, or the factuality, of these events in the early chapters of Genesis. Do you remember, for example, that on one occasion, as so often happened in the course of his ministry, some men came to him trying to 'catch him out' and trip him up, and cause him to do something that would alienate people from him? The Pharisees came, 'tempting him, and saying unto him, Is it lawful for a man to put away his wife for every cause?' (Matthew 19:3).

The Pharisees were divided into two groups. Some said you could put away your wife for more or less any cause. You could have a divorce if you just didn't fancy her; you just had to go through the legal rigmarole and get rid of her and get another wife. Others were much stricter than that. They taught that a divorce could be granted only under certain specific conditions. The Pharisees were therefore putting Christ on the spot when they asked, 'Is it lawful for a man to put away his wife for every cause?' That particular issue need not detain us now. What is significant is the way in which the Lord Jesus Christ uses the Genesis record in his reply:

> And he answered and said unto them, Have ye not read, that he which made them at the beginning made them male and female, and said, For this cause shall a man

leave father and mother, and shall cleave to his wife: and they twain shall be one flesh? Wherefore they are no more twain, but one flesh. What therefore God hath joined together, let not man put asunder (Matthew 19:3-6).

This is actually a quotation from the end of the second chapter of Genesis:

And Adam said, This is now bone of my bones, and flesh of my flesh: she shall be called Woman, because she was taken out of Man. Therefore shall a man leave his father and his mother, and shall cleave unto his wife: and they shall be one flesh (Genesis 2:23-24).

Our Lord Jesus Christ is here undergirding the historicity of the incidents recorded in the early chapters of Genesis. Indeed, it does not stop there. You can go through all the things that modern man finds it most difficult to believe in: the Flood, for example, that terrible judgment of God that fell upon mankind; or the destruction of Sodom and Gomorrah. Did our Lord dismiss those things as fairy stories, as myths? No! He argued that as it happened then, so shall it happen in the day of the Son of Man. In other words, the Lord Jesus Christ had no difficulty in believing that these things really happened.

But before you respond that 'He was just a man of his time, wasn't he?', consider this. Is that what you really think of Jesus Christ, the incarnate Son of God, the one of whom it was said, 'Never man spake like this man', the one who had absolute and perfect knowledge, the one who never spoke a lie, the one who never committed a sin? Are you happy to say that *he* was just a man of his day, in order to justify your arrogant dismissal of these portions of the Word of God?

You can add to that the teaching of the apostles in the New Testament. The whole basis of the second half of Romans chapter 5 rests upon the facts of Genesis 3. Paul draws a great comparison between Adam and Christ. He draws a picture of the whole of mankind being summed up in the headship of Adam. When Adam fell into sin, Paul says, the whole of mankind was involved in that sin. That is Paul's explanation, the Bible's explanation, for the world being as it is, the reason why you and I do not have to learn how to sin. Sinning comes to us instinctively, by nature. All that we have learned is how to sin a little more subtly, a little more cleverly (as we think), in the hope of being able to deceive some other human beings. And we may have foolishly thought that we would be able to deceive God as well. Sin is inherent in men and women, as they are born now, because of what happened here in the Garden of Eden.

The apostle Paul views redeemed humanity as in the Lord Jesus Christ. He says that just as man fell in Adam, so in Christ he is redeemed. He puts before us, if you like, a question: 'Where are you at this moment? Are you in Adam or are you in Christ?' He does the same thing in 1 Corinthians 15: 'For as in Adam all die, even so in Christ shall all be made alive' (verse 22). So you really cannot argue from the Scriptures that these chapters are not historical, that they do not matter, and that they just contain some spiritual truths wrapped up in mythological language. We are dealing here with stark history, and that is why it is so important.

The origin of sin
What is it that happened? In those verses that occur at the opening of the chapter, the serpent comes—no ordinary

snake, of course, but Satan himself. The identification is made exact and specific in the very last book of the Bible, the book of the Revelation. In the twelfth chapter Satan is given some of his names and titles, and these make everything plain: 'And the great dragon was cast out, that old *serpent,* called the Devil, and Satan, which deceiveth the whole world: he was cast out into the earth, and his angels were cast out with him' (Revelation 12:9). And the apostle Paul in 2 Corinthians makes the same identification as he reasons with the Christians in the church at Corinth. He says: 'But I fear, lest by any means, as the *serpent* beguiled Eve through his subtilty, so your minds should be corrupted from the simplicity that is in Christ' (2 Corinthians 11:3). This is no ordinary serpent. This is Satan using a serpent, enabling a serpent to do what serpents are not able to do, to speak and to talk with Eve, the mother of all living as she was to become (Genesis 3: 20).

The serpent comes to her. Eve should have reacted immediately against him, knowing that this sort of thing does not happen. But the serpent speaks and asks her a question. He seems so very reasonable and circumspect in his approach: 'Yea, hath God said, Ye shall not eat of every tree of the garden?' (Genesis 3:1). You notice the hint, the suggestion there. 'Is not this a little bit unreasonable of God, putting a prohibition on every tree in the garden? That is taking it a bit far, isn't it?' Eve knows the truth, because God has spoken the truth. She says: 'We may eat of the fruit of the trees of the garden: but of the fruit of the tree which is in the midst of the garden, God hath said, Ye shall not eat of it, neither shall ye touch it, lest ye die' (Genesis 3:2-3). (God had not said, 'neither shall ye touch it'; he had said that they were not to eat of it.) So Eve was under no misunderstanding as to what God had said, nor therefore as to what were both her responsibility and her duty. Back Satan comes: 'And the serpent said unto the woman, Ye shall not surely die: for God doth know that in the day ye eat thereof, then your eyes shall be opened, and ye shall be as gods, knowing good and evil' (Genesis 3:4-5).

It sounded so plausible. The woman looks at this particular tree—tradition has tried to make out that it was an apple tree, but the Word of God does not say that, nor does it identify it in terms of its type. It is described to us as 'the tree of the knowledge of good and evil'. The woman looks at this tree and the fruit. And when she 'saw that the tree was good for food, and that it was pleasant to the eyes, and a tree to be desired to make one wise, she took of the fruit thereof, and did eat'. That was not the Fall; the Fall comes later. Eve goes to her husband and speaks to him and gives him the fruit. 'Look! Here is the fruit of the tree that God told us not to eat of. I have been speaking with the serpent and the serpent has persuaded me. I have tasted it and it is very nice. Have a bite, Adam!' Adam does exactly what she says, and at that moment man is in a state of rebellion against God—'as in Adam all die'. The New Testament makes it quite clear that there is a sense in which the woman was deceived, tricked, hoodwinked by Satan. Adam was not; he went into it with his eyes wide open. He knew what God had said, and he knew that what the woman had done was wrong; but he identifies himself with her in rebellion against God—and in that moment mankind fell, with tragic consequences. A great Welsh hymn by William Williams, translated by Bobi Jones, sums up the tragedy:

> In Eden—sad indeed that day—
> My countless blessings fled away,
> My crown fell in disgrace.

This is why these events are recorded for us so exactly and meticulously. Here is the origin of sin in the world. This is why the world is as it is now, and why even little babies do not have to be taught how to sin. That is why, however intelligent and intellectual men become, they still have this corrupt heart of sin within them, and they do things (even the most brilliant of them) that are scarcely removed from the activity of beasts. You might argue that it is incredible, it is irrational—and so it is. Men do it because they are sinners; and they are sinners because the Fall took place so long ago, there in the Garden of Eden.

The consequences of sin
We see some of the consequences of sin so clearly depicted for us in this chapter. What does sin do first of all? It immediately cuts a man off from God. It seems to have been the case that God was in the habit—we can only speculate how—of coming down to the Garden of Eden and communing with Adam and Eve. At the evening time on that sad day when they rebelled against God, God comes down. He knows what has happened, and he comes down. 'And they heard the voice of the LORD God walking in the garden in the cool of the day' (Genesis 3:8). Adam and his wife did something that they had never done before. They hid themselves from God. For the first time they knew a craven fear of God in their hearts. It had never happened before; there had been unbroken, unhindered fellowship between them and God. God had given them the instructions—Adam was to keep and tend the garden. God had given him his wife, this woman Eve, and there was unity and harmony between them and God. But now that harmony is sundered, and when God comes, man flees away—he tries to hide from God. He has been doing it ever since. Perhaps you are

trying to do this. You are trying to put a screen between yourself and God. You are looking for a tree to crouch behind, thinking that this will prevent God from seeing and having dealings with you! But this is an impossibility.

Here God comes and calls to Adam, saying to him, 'Where art thou?' Adam, exposed before God, begins to try to make an excuse. 'And he said, I heard thy voice in the garden, and I was afraid, because I was naked; and I hid myself. And he said, Who told thee that thou wast naked? Hast thou eaten of the tree, whereof I commanded thee that thou shouldest not eat? And the man said'—and here you see the next consequence of sin—'The woman whom thou gavest to be with me, she gave me of the tree, and I did eat' (Genesis 3:10-12). Don't blame me, Lord! What do you expect me as a very dutiful and loving husband to do but to join her? It is her fault! Her fault! If she had not done it, I would not have done it. She was the one who took the first bite of the fruit and then she came to me. What could you expect me to do but to join her? It is her fault.

There, in the most intimate relationship of all—the husband-wife relationship—strife and discord have entered. Here was Adam trying to pass the buck, putting the blame, the responsibility, onto his wife Eve. It still happens, doesn't it? How many torn and broken marriages are there in our own community? I was looking at some of the statistics for the nation not so very long ago and it is running something like this: for every three marriages there are two divorces, and the ratio is increasing. What on earth is going to become of society if it goes on like that? You can trace it right back to the Garden of Eden—marital discord, strife, animosity, hatred between those who should be loving towards one another. It has entered here, but of course, because of sin, it does not stop here. In our society it extends beyond those who are nearest and dearest to us. It extends out into the world itself and to other men and women. What is the explanation for wars? Doesn't it come right back to this—animosity, jealousy, antagonism, selfishness—wanting things for yourself and not wanting to pay the price for them? It all comes back to this rebellion against God, there in the Garden of Eden.

> And I will put enmity between thee and the woman, and between thy seed and her seed; it shall bruise thy head, and thou shalt bruise his heel. Unto the woman he said, I will greatly multiply thy sorrow and thy conception; in sorrow thou shalt bring forth children; and thy desire shall be to thy husband, and he shall rule over thee (Genesis 3:15-16).

Why is it, for example, that we live in an age in which Women's Lib, as it is called, has asserted itself? I have got no great time for it, but one can understand to a certain extent why it has come about. It is a reaction against a wrong attitude to women. Go anywhere in the world and you find, especially in societies far removed from any Christian influence, that women are downtrodden. They are looked upon as goods and chattels. You can even see it as you watch some of the immigrants to our country walking along the street, and their womenfolk walking five or six paces behind them. It is as if they do not belong together in the way that should be the case with a husband and wife. It is part of the consequence of sin.

It does not stop even there. You remember that God goes on to speak to Adam, and he says this:

> Because thou hast hearkened unto the voice of thy wife, and hast eaten of the tree, of which I commanded thee,

saying, Thou shalt not eat of it: cursed is the ground for thy sake; in sorrow shalt thou eat of it all the days of thy life; thorns also and thistles shall it bring forth to thee; and thou shalt eat the herb of the field; in the sweat of thy face shalt thou eat bread, till thou return unto the ground (Genesis 3:17-19).

In other words, the very natural order in which we live, the ecological climate of this planet, is disordered, put out of joint, because of man's sin. There is a passage in Romans 8 where the apostle Paul is looking forward to that great time when the Lord Jesus Christ is going to return and everything is going to be put right. He even speaks there of the present sufferings of the animate and inanimate creation:

For the earnest expectation of the creature waiteth for the manifestation of the sons of God. For the creature was made subject to vanity, not willingly, but by reason of him who hath subjected the same in hope, because the creature itself also shall be delivered from the bondage of corruption into the glorious liberty of the children of God. For we know that the whole creation groaneth and travaileth in pain together until now (Romans 8:19-22).

The world of nature round about us has, for all its beauty, an ugliness about it. Nature is 'red in tooth and claw', as the poet Tennyson put it. Natural disasters, floods, famines—even when they are not caused by human sin—have come because of this initial act of man rebelling against God. That is why this is such an important chapter in the unfolding story of God's revelation to us in the Bible. Man has rebelled against God, and man is living with the consequences.

And that is not all. Man is *dying* with the consequences. I did not quite complete what it was that God said to Adam: 'In the sweat of thy face shalt thou eat bread, till thou return unto the ground; for out of it wast thou taken: for dust thou art, and unto dust shalt thou return' (Genesis 3:19). Death was unknown till man sinned. You and I one day, unless the Lord Jesus should return before, will die. We die because we are sinners. And sin entered the world here, in the Garden of Eden, in the way described in this third chapter of Genesis. God had warned Adam, 'for in the day that thou eatest thereof thou shalt surely die' (Genesis 2:17). I know that it was to be many years after this that Adam was to die physically—but he was dead spiritually. The union between him and God was sundered. You may be alive physically and yet dead spiritually; and one day, unless the grace of God intervenes, not only will you be dead physically, but you will linger in spiritual death throughout eternity.

God judges sin
Here then is a chapter of Scripture that enables us to understand this. And surely it says something else to us—something that men do not want to hear, but something that is indelibly written in the story of Scripture. It is this: sin matters to God. God does not wink his eye at sin and pretend it is not there. God deals with sin. In fact, the biblical word that is used for the manner or the method in which God deals with sin is the word 'judgment'. That is what you see beginning to be operated here in this third chapter of Genesis. The woman is judged. The serpent is judged. Adam is judged. Judgment begins to take place. It is but a forerunner, of course, of that great, last, final judgment that shall one day break upon this world when the Lord Jesus Christ returns. God does not trifle with sin. God does not

pretend that it is not there. Sin is an offence to God. Sin is man and woman raising their fists, shaking them in the face of God, and saying, 'We don't want you. We want to go our own way. We prefer it as we are. We don't need you. We don't like you. We find your laws irksome. We are going to break them.' Sin, the New Testament tells us, is rebellion. Sin is lawlessness. Whenever you sin, that is what you are doing; you are acting as a rebellious subject against God, against the one who rules over you. You are telling him that you do not want him and you will not have him.

Well, it's my responsibility to tell you that he will have the last word. God judges sin. No sinner escapes with impunity. There is only one way in which sin can be dealt with, if it is not to be judged in the person of the one who has committed that sin. The great message of the Bible is to tell us how that other way is possible—the way of the cross, for which the Son of God came into the world. This important chapter tells us that because man has rebelled against God, because man is in a state of sin, he has been shut out of Paradise. You notice how his exclusion is underlined in the closing verses:

> Behold, the man is become as one of us, to know good and evil: and now, lest he put forth his hand, and take also of the tree of life, and eat, and live for ever: therefore the LORD God sent him forth from the garden of Eden, to till the ground from whence he was taken. So he drove out the man; and he placed at the east of the garden of Eden Cherubims, and a flaming sword which turned every way, to keep the way of the tree of life (Genesis 3:22-24).

You see, there were two trees—one was forbidden, the other was not. The tree of the knowledge of good and evil was the one that was forbidden. There was also the tree of life; and had they kept God's word, and not partaken of the tree of the knowledge of good and evil, Adam and Eve would have been entitled to eat of the tree of life and live for ever. Having disobeyed God in that one respect, they had forfeited all right to eat of the tree of life. So God guards against anybody coming and partaking of that tree of life. He puts these heavenly creatures, the cherubim, together with a flaming sword, at the entrance to the Garden of Eden. And man is unable again to penetrate the garden. He is expelled—excluded from the presence of God. He will seek vainly and hopelessly to re-enter Paradise, but the way to it is shut and barred—guarded by the angels of God.

What man has been doing ever since is to try and get back to that state of Paradise. Of course he does not pay heed to God, or attempt to get there in the way that he has prescribed. He wants to get there by his own efforts. It is typical of the modern world, isn't it? There is great confidence in man, great emphasis on education, science and all the wonders that modern man can accomplish through his great intellect. You listen to some people and you think that the kingdom of God is going to come upon earth because of man's intelligence. Yet, if you look at some of the very people who make some amazing discovery, you find that their own moral lives are wrecks. They are in ruins, unable to control their own lusts and passions. Having rejected God, they are just reaping the consequences of their sin. Their quest, therefore, be it through science or education, is vain.

Politics never brings in the kingdom of God either. Earlier in this century, here and in other countries, people believed that politicians were able to bring about a just and harmonious society, getting rid of all inequalities, troubles, and distinctions, and that we could have Paradise on earth—Paradise regained, as it were. What has this century seen? Two terrible world wars, as well as many other wars. Mass annihilation through the terrible weapons man's ingenuity has invented! No diminution in crime or injustice; instead, they seem to be increasing. Governments come, governments go; one lot says one thing, another lot says another thing. None are able to bring in heaven upon earth. And none will be able to bring in heaven upon earth, because there are the cherubim with the flaming sword guarding the way to the tree of life, and man as a sinner cannot penetrate back into Paradise. This is a vain and a hopeless quest. But man goes on in his own headstrong, rebellious way, refusing to submit himself to God.

The only way back

Do you know the only way back? It is not the way of man's effort but the way of God's grace. You read about the tree of life again in the last chapter of the Word of God, at the opposite end of the Bible:

And he shewed me a pure river of water of life, clear as crystal, proceeding out of the throne of God and of the Lamb. In the midst of the street of it, and on either side of the river, was there the tree of life, which bare twelve manner of fruits, and yielded her fruit every month: and the leaves of the tree were for the healing of the nations. And there shall be no more curse: but the throne of God and of the Lamb shall be in it; and his servants shall serve him: and they shall see his face; and his name shall be in their foreheads. And there shall be no night there; and they need no candle, neither light of the sun; for the Lord God giveth them light: and they shall reign for ever and ever. And he said unto me, These sayings are faithful and true: and the Lord God of the holy prophets sent his angel to shew unto his servants the things which must shortly be done. Behold, I come quickly: blessed is he that keepeth the sayings of the prophecy of this book (Revelation 22:1-7).

You read later on in the chapter: 'Blessed are they that do his commandments, that they may have right to the tree of life, and may enter in through the gates into the city.' The way to that tree of life, the way into the city of God, the way into the kingdom of God, comes through the one who is spoken of in this chapter. In the judgment that was passed upon Satan, God says this: 'And I will put enmity between thee and the woman, and between thy seed and her seed; it shall bruise thy head, and thou shalt bruise his heel' (Genesis: 3:15).

Who is the seed of the woman? The Lord Jesus Christ, the One who came from heaven to undo the devastation brought upon mankind by Adam's sin. He came; Satan did his utmost against him; but all that Satan could do was to bruise his heel. On the cross the Lord Jesus Christ had the victory. I have already quoted from William Williams' hymn:

> In Eden—sad indeed that day—
> My countless blessings fled away,
> My crown fell in disgrace.

It goes on to speak about a great conflict taking place upon the cross. There were two there—Christ and the serpent—and they fought:

> Though two had wounds, there conquered One—
> And Jesus was His Name.

The way back to Paradise, the only entrance to Paradise, is through that Son of God, the Lord Jesus Christ, and through faith in him. He had to deal with this terrible problem of sin. He came and dealt with it by taking it to himself, so that he, who was sinless, was looked upon by his own Father as the vilest sinner in the world. This terrible judgment of God fell on him as the substitute—the Lamb of God slain from the foundation of the world. The word of the gospel is that any sinner, however dire his sins, if he turns to that Saviour, Jesus Christ, and trusts in him, has his sins washed away. That person is given the right to enter the kingdom of God, the city of God—to become a partaker of the fruit of the tree of life and, for ever and for ever in eternity, to be there in God's presence.

That is why this chapter is so important. Without it you do not understand the Bible; you do not understand the world; you do not understand yourself. But with it, you are not only given understanding; you are given hope; you are given the way of salvation. You are given this great message of a God of grace and mercy, who sent his Son on his great rescue mission to save sinners like you and me! Is he your Saviour? Whom do you line up with—rebellious Adam, Satan, or the Lord Jesus Christ? That is the choice before you. God grant that you will come and trust in Jesus.

Chapter Two
Man's only hope in evil times

And to Seth, to him also there was born a son;
and he called his name Enos: then began men to
call upon the name of the LORD.
(Genesis 4:26)

I am sure that these particular verses are not often read in public worship, and that those in the habit of reading their Bibles do not habitually turn to the fourth chapter of Genesis! If we are in need of comfort, encouragement or guidance, we probably turn to one of the Gospels, or one of the Epistles, or one of the Psalms—but not to Genesis 4. This chapter, as it begins to record what happened to the descendants of Adam and Eve, gives us some very strange facts. The previous chapter, as we have seen, describes how man, who had been created in a state of perfection and innocence, by his act of flagrant rebellion against God brought down upon himself, the whole creation, and all his descendants, the judgment of God. It ends by telling how God expelled Adam and Eve from the Garden of Eden and set there cherubim, heavenly creatures, with a flaming sword to guard the entrance into the Garden of Eden, lest the man should come again and partake of the tree of life. He was now alienated from God. Having made his choice deliberately and freely, he now had to take the consequences. The events recorded here in chapter 4 follow immediately.

31

We are all familiar with the opening passage of this fourth chapter: Cain and Abel—the first murder recorded in Scripture! Here are two brothers, sons of Adam and Eve, one a 'keeper of sheep' and the other a 'tiller of the ground'. They brought their offerings to the Lord, and we are told that the Lord had respect to the offering that Abel brought to him, but he did not have respect to Cain's offering. The offering of Abel, as the epistle to the Hebrews (11:4) makes clear, was presented in faith; whereas it appears that Cain's offering was brought in self-confidence before God—and such an attitude is never acceptable to him. So a spirit of envy arises in the heart of Cain towards Abel, culminating in the terrible act that he commits. He takes his brother into the field and, while they are talking, he sets upon him and kills him.

The chapter then tells how God dealt with Cain. God did not annihilate Cain. He might have done so, for God was perfectly capable of intervening in a dramatic and decisive way and smiting down this man who had the temerity to slay his brother. But he did not do that. Instead, he engaged in a dialogue with him. But Cain is quite unrepentant. 'Am I my brother's keeper?' he arrogantly asks, in reply to God's question 'Where is Abel thy brother?' Instead of being subjected to the death penalty, as might well have been the case, Cain is condemned to wander through the earth. A mark is put on him, a mark to preserve him from the vengeance of other men.

The remainder of the chapter, until the last couple of verses, is taken up with an account of Cain's descendants. We are told of the sons that he had, and then of the sons that they had, and of some of the events in their lives. The story unfolds as the developing picture of the history of the world. At the end of the chapter there comes this statement:

'then began men to call upon the name of the LORD' (verse 26). It was not one of the descendants of Cain who began to do that. Instead, Adam and Eve had another child whose name was Seth, and Seth in turn had a son whose name was Enos. The Bible then says, 'then began men to call upon the name of the LORD'.

A melancholy refrain

The fifth chapter, which speaks of the amazing ages to which these early men lived, brings out the fact that *they all died*. Indeed, in the course of these verses it recurs almost like a monotonous and impelling refrain. Adam died; each of them died; they all died. We are given an account of how long they lived, how old they were when they died, when they had their respective children, and how long they lived after that. Then comes that sad, melancholy refrain—'*and he died*'.

The first question that naturally arises from such a passage is this: Why was it recorded? Why is it that it comes here? Why is it in Scripture at all? In part, the answer is the same as I gave to a similar question about Genesis chapter 3—it happened! We are not dealing here with mythology; we are dealing with history—which is one reason why you are given the number of years these men lived. It may be far removed from what we are used to, but trace it on through Scripture and you discover that the number of years to which men and women live seems to diminish and diminish. But here, right at the beginning of Scripture, they live an almost incredible length of time—eight hundred years and, some of them, over nine hundred years. But then they died. I say it runs throughout like a melancholy refrain. You could read almost the whole of the fifth chapter and the story would be the same. It is recorded, first of all, because it happened.

Yet that is an insufficient answer to the question, Why is *this* recorded? We are not told of many of the things that happened to the men in this chapter, so why are we given this picture of the way things went after the sin of Adam and Eve? The answer is that God is seeking to show what happens when man turns away from him. Back in the Garden of Eden, when God came down and visited Adam and Eve and spoke with them, he began to pronounce on them and Satan the words of judgment that the third chapter contains. He indicated to Adam, 'dust thou art, and unto dust shalt thou return' (Genesis 3:19). That, in effect, was an echo of the threat recorded for us in the second chapter of the book of Genesis, where God had told Adam that 'in the day that thou eatest thereof thou shalt surely die' (Genesis 2:17). Of course, he did die spiritually at the very moment he partook of that food. He was separated from God—no longer in the state of fellowship with God that he had known since the moment of his creation. God was now his adversary. He was alienated from God; but he was not yet dead physically. Indeed it would be many hundreds of years before he would die physically. This chapter begins to open to us the story, not just of a man and a woman in sin, but the story of humankind, of society in sin—the sad story of what happens to the whole of mankind now that it is alienated from God.

You notice that something is true of all the sons of all the children of Adam and Eve. They are all sinners; not one of them is born in a state of innocence. That is expressed for us, of course, most clearly and succinctly in the New Testament, where the apostle Paul tells us very plainly: 'For all have sinned, and come short of the glory of God' (Romans 3:23); 'There is none righteous, no, not one' (Romans 3:10). The same apostle declares that 'in Adam all die' (1 Corinthians 15:22). Here, in the history given to us in Genesis 4, we see this melancholy story of death reaping its vengeful reward upon men because they are sinners. Men die because they are rebels against God.

But apart from the murder of Abel, and another instance when Lamech boasts about a murder that he has committed, you do not read of death as such in chapter 4: that is, of what coroners call 'death from natural causes'. Instead, what you are given, after the account of Abel's murder by his brother Cain and God's word of judgment upon Cain, is a picture of life developing, of society developing—if you like, of all civilisation developing. I want you to banish from your minds the idea of a primitive 'Stone-Age man' which you might have imbibed from a schoolteacher who was under the illusion that he was teaching you history when he put such nonsense into your mind. That is not the picture we are given here. Here man, as it were, is only one stage removed from the creature that God has made in a state of perfection. Sin had begun to wreak havoc in his life, but it had not reached the stage that it has now reached in the world. Who knows what lies hidden behind some of the phrases that describe to us the achievements of these sons and grandsons whose names are recorded for us in this chapter? I think we are intended to understand that here is a society that is developing in various ways and is very proud of its accomplishments. There is satisfaction and delight in what it is achieving. That is the sort of picture we are given.

A developing society

Let me explain what I mean in a little more detail. Did you notice what Cain does when he goes out from the presence of God, condemned to be a fugitive and a vagabond in the earth? What he does, in a sense, is to shake his fist in God's face: 'I'm not going to be a fugitive and a vagabond', he says; 'I'm going to have a settled existence. I'm going to live in a city!' (A city was probably some kind of fortified settlement.) In this he felt that he would be secure. 'And Cain went out from the presence of the LORD, and dwelt in the land of Nod, on the east of Eden. And Cain knew his wife; and she conceived, and bare Enoch: and he builded a city, and called the name of the city, after the name of his son, Enoch' (Genesis 4:16-17). Here you see that people were coming together, for obviously there were other sons and daughters of Adam and Eve alive at this time. That is how the human race was propagated in those early days. They are beginning to have some sort of communal existence. It is not just the family—father, mother and the immediate children—but more and more are being gathered into this society until you have what is called here a city.

It does not stop there. After a generation or so you come on to Lamech. 'And Lamech took unto him two wives: the name of the one was Adah, and the name of the other Zillah. And Adah bare Jabal: he was the father of such as dwell in tents, and of such as have cattle' (Genesis 4:19-20). We are given the names of the wives of Lamech and the names of their children; and then we are given a picture of a whole group of men who are skilled in rearing cattle. In another branch of the human family very different skills were being developed, for we read: 'And his brother's name was Jubal: he was the father of all such as handle the harp and organ' (Genesis 4:21). Here is a developing culture. Music! People are able to make and play instruments—not just one, but more than one—and obviously they are getting enjoyment and pleasure out of it. So here is another branch of society, with skills in that direction.

There is more fascinating detail to come. 'And Zillah, she also bare Tubalcain, an instructer of every artificer in brass and iron: and the sister of Tubalcain was Naamah' (Genesis 4:22). Could we put it like this? Here are the beginnings of what today is called industry. They are able to produce metals, and they are able to work upon them and fashion implements from them. Here is progress! That is surely how they would have described it. Did poor old Adam have any implements made of metal to help him do his gardening? They would probably have looked upon their progress much as we look upon the progress of our day. It is a picture of society developing in every way: plenty of food, work, pleasure—everything, you might argue, that one needs for a successful and happy existence.

You can add to that something else that becomes apparent in this chapter. Look at this man Lamech—what does he do? He is not content with one wife; he takes two wives. We are given their names: one was Adah, the other was Zillah. This is something that is against the will of God, for in Genesis 2 monogamy is very clearly instituted and established by God. 'And Adam said, This is now bone of my bones, and flesh of my flesh: she shall be called Woman, because she was taken out of Man. Therefore shall a man leave his father and his mother, and shall cleave unto his wife: and they shall be one flesh' (Genesis 2:23-24). In other words, there is something exclusive about this relationship. A man can only be one flesh with *one* woman. He cannot have a whole series of wives and in that sense be in equal standing with each of them. But this man Lamech does not bother about things like that. He has one wife; he wants another; so he takes her and we are given the account of that very fact.

What I am pointing out is this. We are given in this

chapter an account, in microcosm, of the unfolding development of the human race. Indeed there is something exceptionally modern about this chapter. Take the various things that I have mentioned—don't they form an essential part of many people's lives today? Were you to ask them what is needed for a happy and fulfilled existence here upon earth, many would answer you in terms of this chapter. They would say that a man needs food, enjoyment, a bit of culture—the arts, music, drama, whatever it is. Or, at a more popular level, he needs a television set in the corner of his house, so that he is able to turn it on and have his little bit of culture coming into his own home. Then, as well as that, modern man needs industry. And he needs sex, doesn't he? That is all the rage in these days. No restraints, no limitations; if you want it, you take it. Lamech is a very modern man!

In other words, like so many parts of Scripture when you read it with insight and understanding, this chapter is not just telling you about something that happened many thousands of years ago—it *is* doing that, but it is not simply doing that. It is also saying, Do you not see *our* society in this? Do you not see that here is a mirror to the world—that this is the way the world goes? It is not quite as old, but almost as old, as creation. These are the things that men want and grasp after and strive for. These are the things that men think will bring them satisfaction.

Do you notice something else about this man Lamech? It does not come across very clearly in the English, but it is there very clearly in the Hebrew. He begins to sing, and he is singing to his wives of sin. 'And Lamech said unto his wives, Adah and Zillah, Hear my voice; ye wives of Lamech, hearken unto my speech: for I have slain a man to my wounding, and a young man to my hurt' (Genesis 4:23).

This is poetry, but Hebrew poetry does not rhyme and scan as poetry does in English. It makes great use of parallelism:

> I have slain a man to my wounding,
>   and a young man to my hurt.
> If Cain shall be avenged sevenfold,
>   truly Lamech seventy and sevenfold.

In other words, what Lamech is doing is flaunting himself in the face of God. 'I have killed a man,' he says, 'and nothing has happened to me!' He is thinking back to his ancestor Cain. Do you remember what God said about Cain? There was going to be a mark upon him to preserve him; if anybody exercised vengeance on Cain, sevenfold vengeance would be exercised against him. 'Well,' says Lamech, 'I've killed a man and it's not sevenfold vengeance. It's seventy times seven! What is God going to do about it? Who is God? What is all this business about death?'

A deteriorating society

So the chapter is describing the unfolding story of man in his arrogance. Rebelling against God, he thinks that he is getting away scot-free before God. In fact, as you read through this chapter, once you have passed the acceptable offering that Abel made to God, it is not until the very last verse that you read anything about a man with a sense of his need of God. That is why a chapter like this is so exceedingly modern. Here they have everything. They have their agriculture, their industry, their arts and culture and the rest of it—but they have the sad features of civilisation as well. They have their violence and murder and adultery and all the suffering that comes from that. But any thought of God? No!

Yet Adam and Eve were still alive at this time—Adam and Eve who had known personal dealings with God, and who were able to tell these people the real truth about God. But it is as if the people have just shrugged their shoulders and brushed it all to one side. 'Who needs God? We have got food, we have got work, we have got pleasure, we have got sex, and if somebody comes against us we will deal with him. Who is going to come and overpower us? What do we need God for? What was it that God was supposed to have said to you, Adam—"in the day that thou eatest thereof thou shalt surely die"? And how many hundreds of years ago was that? You are still alive and walking the face of the earth. The only men who have died are the men who died violently at the hands of other men. This business about death really does not bear examination!'

So God has been rejected. God has been repudiated. God has been totally ignored. Very modern, isn't it? We live in a society that has been doing that increasingly, and that is why I call your attention to this particular passage of Scripture. It gives to us in many ways an exact replica of the development of our modern society. You see, once individuals or societies turn away from God they do not stand still. They do not remain in the condition that prevailed before they turned their backs on God. Immediately life begins to deteriorate. You get sin piling upon sin; more violent sin coming upon more violent sin—until you come to this arrogant man Lamech's cry, taunting God as he sings this little bit of poetry to his wives. He more or less says, 'Who can touch me? I've killed men. I've killed a young man. I was wounded, but I won the fight. Who's able to overcome me?' In this appalling deterioration of society God does not come into the picture at all. God, in a sense, is not simply allowing this to happen, but by the withdrawing of his presence he is almost constraining society to go in this way.

In many ways a perfect parallel to this is given to us in the New Testament in the epistle to the Romans. Paul, writing of the corrupt and cruel society of the age in which he lived, gives an excellent explanation of what had happened. He is speaking of the gospel and why the gospel is necessary.

> For the wrath of God is revealed from heaven against all ungodliness and unrighteousness of men, who hold the truth in unrighteousness; because that which may be known of God is manifest in them; for God hath shewed it unto them. For the invisible things of him from the creation of the world are clearly seen, being understood by the things that are made, even his eternal power and Godhead; so that they are without excuse (Romans 1:18-20).

Like the people in Genesis 4, the people of Paul's day should have reasoned to the conclusion that there is a God who is to be worshipped. The heavens above them, the world in which they lived, spoke in eloquent testimony of the fact of the Creator, an almighty, powerful, sovereign Creator who is to be worshipped. But they did not bother. The apostle goes on to say:

> Because that, when they knew God, they glorified him not as God, neither were thankful; but became vain in their imaginations, and their foolish heart was darkened. Professing themselves to be wise, they became fools, and changed the glory of the uncorruptible God into an image made like to corruptible man, and to birds, and to fourfooted beasts, and creeping things (Romans 1:21-23).

Paul is speaking of his own age, of the Romans and the

Greeks, those highly intelligent and articulate races. Yet, when it came to worshipping God, what did they do? They thought of a concept of love, or power, or justice, and they carved a piece of wood or stone and put a name under it and said, 'That is the god of justice; that is the god of love; that is the god of power; that is the god of revenge', and so on! You name it and they had a god or goddess for it. They did not even use their God-given intelligence to realise that if they had carved those things, how could they be gods? How could they be the One who had created all things? 'And their foolish heart was darkened. Professing themselves to be wise, they became fools.' And so we go on:

> Wherefore God also gave them up to uncleanness through the lusts of their own hearts, to dishonour their own bodies between themselves: who changed the truth of God into a lie, and worshipped and served the creature more than the Creator, who is blessed for ever. Amen. For this cause God gave them up unto vile affections: for even their women did change the natural use into that which is against nature: and likewise also the men, leaving the natural use of the woman, burned in their lust one toward another; men with men working that which is unseemly, and receiving in themselves that recompence of their error which was meet. And even as they did not like to retain God in their knowledge, God gave them over to a reprobate mind, to do those things which are not convenient (Romans 1:24-28).

Our modern society

I wonder at the intelligence of anybody who tells me that the Bible does not speak to our modern society. Here you have a description not simply of what was happening in the society of which Paul was a member almost two thousand years ago, but an equally perfect description of modern society. These terrible sins that have broken out in society, in so-called Western civilisation—the homosexuality, the lesbianism—all these are abominations in the sight of God. Man has turned away from God and so God says, 'You want to go that way? Go the way of sin and see where it gets you. See the pleasure that allegedly it gives you. See what it does to your society. You turn from me—I will withdraw myself from you. I will take the restraints off; I will take the brakes off, and you will soon find that sin is carrying you headlong down the slope to hell!'

That is what has been happening in our own nation, in our own society, in the years that have marked our lives. It is all here in principle, back at the beginning of the Bible. Men do not bother with God, so what do they do? They give themselves over to sexual lust, to violence, to murder—even a brother murdering his brother. I won't say that you can justify it, but in one sense you can understand a man murdering someone not related to him, somebody far removed from him, who comes and impinges upon his rights. But here is his innocent brother, and he rises up against him and kills him! I guarantee that in your papers during the coming week you will find things not far removed from this: troubles in families, husbands and wives violent towards one another, sons and fathers fighting and sometimes killing one another. Let nobody say that this old book, the Bible, is out of date and irrelevant! It enables us to understand the world in which we live, and it enables the Christian to be able to speak to this world.

Christians ought at the present time to be asking their fellow human beings who do not claim to be Christians how they account for things as they are in our nation.

Remember that we are not one of the backward nations of the world. We are not people who have just emerged from almost countless centuries of barbarism and cannibalism or anything like that! Yet you could go to many less developed societies and you would find higher moral standards there than you would find in Britain today. I have often spoken with students who come to this country from far-off places to study in our colleges and universities. They have no great tradition of Christianity behind them—perhaps some of them are first- or, at most, second-generation Christians. They touch down in London Airport and they look in the bookstalls, or they go to the hotel and turn on the television, and they see the sex and the violence pouring out. They read the newspapers and they see things that would never be allowed to be printed in their own country. They say, 'Is this Christian Britain? How have things come to this pass? How is it that there's this terrible violence? Why this great multiplication of cases of rape and sexual assault and child abuse?' It is not just that more cases are being reported now than in the past. In all these areas there has been a terrible increase. When I was a boy—and this would be even truer for those older than I am—murder was something that caught the headlines. It did happen, but not to the extent that it happens today. So why is it that we—presumably the heirs of one of the greatest civilisations of all history—are as we are?

Why do you find these things pervading all classes of society? Theoretically it should not happen. Give a man a good education, a comfortable home, enough money to live on—then surely, you might say, he doesn't need to resort to all these things. And yet you know as well as I do that that is the sad story of our society. The humanist cannot explain it—it is really a denial of humanism. The humanist maintains that if you take away a man's disadvantages, if you clothe him, educate him, feed him, give him a bit of freedom, then he will rise up on the ladder of progress. It is almost as if God is saying to man in the Western world in the twentieth century, 'That is the theory of humanism. This is the practice of humanism. This is where it gets you. You turn away from God and your society goes down into the gutter!'

Now that is surely what has been happening in the lifetime of many of us, and with accelerating rapidity during this last quarter of a century. How do you account for it? The humanist cannot account for it: the Christian can. The Christian says that it is because man has turned away from God. Man has determined not to have God in his reckoning, and therefore God gives him up; God abandons him. God says, 'You think you can do without me. Try it and see where it gets you!' Society degenerates and deteriorates. You would think that men would begin to learn the lesson, but they do not. They go on picking on every commandment of the living God and somehow seeking to legislate around it so that it is no longer binding upon them. They excuse sin, they will not call it sin—and all the while society seems to get worse and worse. That is something the Christian understands.

If you are not a Christian, I want you to think very seriously about this case that I am presenting. How do you account for the moral state of Britain? According to all the theories it should not be like this; but you and I know that we are in a desperate condition from a moral and spiritual point of view. The Bible, I say, gives us the perfect answer. Here, near the beginning of the Bible, we are given this instance of what happens when man turns from God. He still progresses—it certainly was progress to have the things mentioned in this chapter—the agricultural developments, the industrial developments, and the cultural developments. In one sense what man was doing, in a perverted way, was to work out something God commanded him to do back in the first chapter of Genesis:

> So God created man in his own image, in the image of God created he him; male and female created he them. And God blessed them, and God said unto them, Be fruitful, and multiply, and replenish the earth, and subdue it: and have dominion over the fish of the sea, and over the fowl of the air, and over every living thing that moveth upon the earth (Genesis 1:27-28).

That was something spoken by God to man when he was in a state of innocence. He was to rule over creation. It is sometimes termed, in a technical phrase, 'the cultural mandate'. Under this term you can put all scientific development, all cultural and artistic development. This mandate declares that ultimately God has given us all things richly to enjoy. He has not made us animals; he has made us human beings. He made us with higher instincts than any animal ever has had or ever will have. He has made us with capabilities and powers of artistic expression and creativity, and he wants us to use them.

That, in a sense, was what happened here in this fourth chapter of Genesis. But the sad fact is that things were being developed without God, away from God, and against God. Go to any of the arts, or any of the aspects of culture in modern society, and you do not see the hand of God in them. You pick up a novel. Are you cleaner when you have finished reading it? Are you brought closer to God? Or have you learned of a few sins that perhaps you were less aware of when you started reading it? You watch a film or a chat show on the television. Is your soul elevated? Or does dirt come out of the screen and smear itself over your soul? Isn't it like that? Do you listen much to modern music? Does it give you peace? Does it give you a sense of God and truth and holiness? Isn't there something ugly about so much of it, a battering of your senses as it pounds its message into you, a message of meaninglessness, a message that is anti-God? The tragedy is that so many people think that that is music. They don't know what beauty is, they don't know what harmony is, because so much modern music deliberately sets itself to destroy these. Culture in rebellion against God! You can go into the realm of art and look at some of these modern 'artistic' productions, and are they really worth the name? Statues, works of art, paintings—you look at them and you say, Where is the beauty? Where is the sense of balance and proportion? There is simply ugliness there, the equivalent of the discord and the strife that you hear in much music. It comes across to you visually and you realise that here is another area of culture in rebellion against God. It is the same in the realm of drama. God is ignored, and if he is mentioned it is only to be mocked, in order that men might set themselves against him. His mercy, his compassion, his love, his kindness are not presented. Instead, you find expressed man's arrogant rebellion against God. The whole of our society is shaking its fist in the face of Almighty God. Is it any wonder that things deteriorate and get worse and worse by the day? Here it is, in principle, almost at the beginning of the Bible.

A landmark of hope
Then something happens. Adam and Eve have another son. His name is Seth. He is going to be very important—

indeed, much of the next chapter of Scripture is taken up with the story of his descendants. He becomes a very important figure in the ongoing story of the redemptive purposes of God in Scripture. We are told: 'And Adam knew his wife again; and she bare a son, and called his name Seth: For God, said she, hath appointed me another seed instead of Abel, whom Cain slew. And to Seth, to him also there was born a son; and he called his name Enos: then began men to call upon the name of the LORD' (Genesis 4:25-26).

In a society that was hostile, godless and arrogant in its hostility to God, here was a man who began to 'call upon the name of the Lord'. This phrase means to pray—to cry out to God, 'Lord, help me! Lord, deliver me!' It's one of the great phrases used in Scripture for poor sinners crying out to God to have mercy on them. This becomes, you might say, the first great spiritual landmark in sinful society. It is the first great landmark of hope from men who are surrounded by sin and are sinners themselves, realising the hopelessness of everything that they can see and crying out to God to help them and to deliver them. And, amazingly, this is just what God is going to do.

The great message of the Bible is that God hears and answers that prayer. God comes and deals mercifully with those who give utterance to such prayer—those that 'call upon the name of the Lord'. Compared with us, you would have to say that this man Seth and his son Enos must have been very ignorant. What did they know, compared with what we know, of God's gracious purposes? All they had was the word of promise that had been given about Eve— a word of judgment, and yet, at the same time, a word of promise. God said to Satan: 'And I will put enmity between thee and the woman, and between thy seed and her seed; it shall bruise thy head, and thou shalt bruise his heel' (Genesis 3:15). It was a promise that from the seed of the woman would come that promised One who would be the great deliverer of the people of God. What a bare word of promise to hold onto! How ignorant must these men have been compared with us! If you have read the Bible, especially the New Testament, you have more knowledge than these men had. Yet you may never have done what they did—they called upon the name of the Lord!

Of course, as we read the unfolding story of Scripture we know who the Lord is. The Lord God sent his Son Jesus Christ into the world. He is the Lord. Those preachers of the gospel who went out from Jerusalem in the first years of the Christian era preached Jesus Christ as Lord. On one occasion the apostle Peter, when hauled before a tribunal and forbidden to preach the gospel, boldly declared that he would not desist from so doing, declaring that 'there is none other name under heaven given among men, whereby we must be saved' (Acts 4:12). He was urging his hearers to call upon the name of the Lord.

Do you remember the incident with which this chapter opened? Cain slaughters his brother Abel—murders him—and the blood of Abel falls into the ground and, as it were, cries out from the ground to God. 'And the LORD said unto Cain, Where is Abel thy brother? And he said, I know not: Am I my brother's keeper? And he said, What hast thou done? the voice of thy brother's blood crieth unto me from the ground' (Genesis 4:9-10). There is a verse in the epistle to the Hebrews that picks this up. The writer tells the Christians, some of whom were thinking of abandoning their faith in Jesus Christ, of all the advantages they have in Jesus. He says: 'And [you have come] to Jesus the mediator of the new covenant, and to the blood of sprinkling, that speaketh better things than that of Abel' (Hebrews 12:24). What was it that Abel's blood cried out for? Revenge. Vengeance. Retribution upon this wicked brother who had slaughtered Abel. That is what the blood of Abel cried out for from the ground. You might say that natural justice demanded it. But for what does the blood of Jesus Christ cry out? It is not revenge; it is mercy, pardon for sinners, and hope for rebels against God. The apostle John says that the blood of Jesus Christ, God's Son, cleanses us from all sin (1 John 1:7)

Although Jesus let men take him and nail him so cruelly to that cross on the hill Calvary, the shedding of his blood is the great means of man's salvation. Do you know the only answer to this world today—just as it was the only answer to the world in which these men in Genesis chapter 4 lived? The only answer is to call upon the name of the Lord, whatever the rest of society might do. No doubt the people laughed at Seth and Enos when they began to hold their prayer meetings and call upon the name of the Lord. But before many years had passed they were to die, and how they must have wished that they had listened! They must have wished then that they had called upon the name of the Lord. When a Christian dies it is not that he fears anything—he knows that he is entering into the very presence of God. The blood of Jesus Christ, God's Son, has cleansed him. The blood of Jesus, the mediator of the new covenant, speaks better things than that of Abel. The Christian knows that by that blood he is ushered into the very presence of God.

Do you trust in the Lord Jesus Christ? Are you still in your sins? Are you part and parcel of this sinking humanity that is all around us—a hopeless, hell-bound society? Or are you willing to do what they will laugh at you for doing?

Are you willing to stand and call upon the name of the Lord? If you do it, salvation is yours. If you do not, you are lost without hope.

Chapter Three
The man who pleased God

And Enoch lived sixty and five years,
and begat Methuselah: and Enoch walked with
God after he begat Methuselah three hundred years,
and begat sons and daughters: and all the days of
Enoch were three hundred sixty and five years: and
Enoch walked with God: and he was not; for God
took him. And Methuselah lived an hundred eighty
and seven years, and begat Lamech.
(Genesis 5:21-25)

By faith Enoch was translated that he should not
see death; and was not found, because God had
translated him: for before his translation he had this
testimony, that he pleased God. But without faith it
is impossible to please him: for he that cometh to
God must believe that he is, and that he is a
rewarder of them that diligently seek him.
(Hebrews 11:5-6)

The first of these passages occurs in a very strange con-text, far removed from anything with which we are familiar. It is what could be called a genealogy, giving us the family tree of a certain line of descendants. At the end of the previous chapter, we read that Adam and Eve had another son called Seth. Genesis 5 is really Seth's family tree; it gives us the various descendants, stretching down to a much more familiar character in Scripture, a man named

Noah. Genesis 5 spans the gap extending through hundreds of years between Seth's birth and the coming of Noah. It is a strange chapter, not least because of the remarkable statistics contained in it. Listen to some of them: 'And the days of Adam after he had begotten Seth were eight hundred years: and he begat sons and daughters: and all the days that Adam lived were nine hundred and thirty years: and he died' (Genesis 5:4-5). That kind of pattern comes like a refrain through the rest of the chapter. 'And Seth lived an hundred and five years, and begat Enos: and Seth lived after he begat Enos eight hundred and seven years, and begat sons and daughters' (Genesis 5:6-7). The same with Enos: '. . . and all the days of Enos were nine hundred and five years: and he died' (Genesis 5:11). Then Cainan, Mahalaleel, Jared, and so on—we are given this precise description of how long they lived, how old they were when they became fathers, how long they lived after that, and then the total number of years that they lived. At the end comes this sad and melancholy refrain, *'and he died'*. The chapter is like that almost from beginning to end.

Then you get the account of the life of Enoch, and it is different. It begins in the same way: 'And Enoch lived sixty and five years, and begat Methuselah' (Genesis 5:21). But then comes the difference: 'And Enoch walked with God after he begat Methuselah three hundred years, and begat sons and daughters' (Genesis 5:22). You would expect the next statement to follow the pattern of the preceding verses, adding the sixty-five and the three hundred years, and stating that Enoch lived for three hundred and sixty-five years and he died. But you do not read that: 'And all the days of Enoch were three hundred sixty and five years: and Enoch walked with God: and he was not; for God took him' (Genesis 5:23-24).

A man who did not die

We have here something almost unique, not simply in Scripture but in the whole of human history. We are faced here with a man who did not die. In 2 Kings 2, we have an account of the one other person in Scripture who did not die—the great prophet of the Lord called Elijah. Instead of dying he was carried up from earth to heaven in a chariot of fire. These are the only two exceptions to the universal story of death.

It is therefore worth while to look at this man Enoch, this almost unique man. Obviously there was something very exceptional, something very special about him. What was it that caused God to come and take Enoch, instead of bringing Enoch to the place of death to which all other men have to come—and through which you and I must one day pass? God took him, or as the writer to the Hebrews puts it, quoting the Greek version of the Old Testament: 'By faith Enoch was translated that he should not see death; and was not found, because God had translated him: for before his translation he had this testimony, that he pleased God' (Hebrews 11:5).

This is obviously something very strange, something unique and remarkable, and therefore worthy of our consideration. So I want us to give our attention to it and see what this man has to say to us. Remember that the New Testament says of the Old Testament scriptures: 'whatsoever things were written aforetime were written for our learning' (Romans 15:4). So there is something for us here in this portion of Scripture. God has caused no part of his Word to be recorded and preserved for us down through the ages in order that we may dismiss it as either unimportant or untruthful. 'All scripture is given by inspiration of God' (2 Timothy 3:16), and the passage we are considering comes under this heading.

Thus we cannot avoid this man. You might say that it would have been easier for me to jump from Genesis 4 to Genesis 6—although 'easier' would be a comparative description, because here we are dealing with those parts of Scripture that modern man finds the most objectionable. I wonder what your reaction is to my text—and to the fact that I insist that we are dealing here with statistics that are to be believed. What we have here is not something fanciful, not something in the realm of mythology that might possibly have a lesson for us akin to those that we derive from fairy stories—but something that is history.

You might ask, 'What on earth makes you think that this is history?' Simply this—as you read through these early chapters of Scripture, you are surely driven to the conclusion that, whatever *you* might think of them, the writer thought that he was writing history. He is careful to record things in detail. He gives us, for example, the specific ages of these men because he believed that it really happened like this. You might say, 'Perhaps *he* believed that, but why should we believe it with all our education? We are people living almost at the end of the twentieth century. You cannot seriously expect us to believe something as primitive as some scholars reckon the book of Genesis to be! Surely this must be ruled out of court!' I want to show you, however, that if you think like that you are making a great mistake. Remember that the Lord Jesus Christ quoted from these early chapters of Genesis more than once, and he alluded to the people mentioned here as historical realities. He had no difficulty in recognising this as sober history.

Let me begin by tackling what is for some the great difficulty of the longevity of these men listed here. What was the life span of Methuselah? 'Nine hundred sixty and nine years!' He was the man who lived longer than anybody else.' Others run him very, very close in this chapter of Scripture. 'How can you believe that something like that ever happened?' someone may ask. First of all, because it is in God's Word and God does not tell lies. That is a sufficient reason, but I want to go on beyond that, because I think that there are very good reasons why one is able to come to a passage like this and not simply dismiss it out of hand.

Before the Flood

Think, for example, of the period of history spoken of in this chapter. This is the period before the Flood, the Antediluvian Period, to give it its correct title. As you read the early chapters of Genesis prior to chapters 6–8 with their detailed account of the Flood, you can be in no doubt that you are dealing with what, in many ways, was a different order of existence from that which we know today. Given that different order of existence, I have no difficulty at all in recognising the historicity of the tremendously long lives lived by these men—seven, eight, nine hundred plus years. It was different in many ways. Let me quote verses from these early chapters, first of all from Genesis 2. God has created all things; he has set man there in the Garden of Eden.

> These are the generations of the heavens and of the earth when they were created, in the day that the LORD God made the earth and the heavens, and every plant of the field before it was in the earth, and every herb of the field before it grew: for the LORD God had not caused it to rain upon the earth, and there was not a man to till the ground. But there went up a mist from the earth, and watered the whole face of the ground (Genesis 2:4-6).

The verses following give a detailed account of the creation of Adam and Eve. But the particular words I want you to consider are these: 'the LORD God had not caused it to rain upon the earth . . . But there went up a mist from the earth, and watered the whole face of the ground.' Also these verses from the previous chapter:

And God said, Let there be a firmament in the midst of the waters, and let it divide the waters from the waters. And God made the firmament, and divided the waters which were under the firmament from the waters which were above the firmament: and it was so. And God called the firmament Heaven. And the evening and the morning were the second day. And God said, Let the waters under the heaven be gathered together unto one place, and let the dry land appear: and it was so. And God called the dry land Earth; and the gathering together of the waters called he Seas: and God saw that it was good (Genesis 1:6-10).

Do you get the picture? In Genesis 1 the story of creation is given. There is the division of the water so that there is water both above and below; and then the water below is gathered together to form the seas and the dry land appears. But still there is a canopy of water over the earth's face. As yet there is no rain. This canopy with mist and water vapour is evidently what was designed to be there. Until the Flood there was no such thing as rain as we know it. Then in Genesis 6 and 7 we are given the account of the Flood. God says: 'For yet seven days, and I will cause it to rain upon the earth forty days and forty nights; and every living substance that I have made will I destroy from off the face of the earth' (Genesis 7:4). And a little later in the chapter: 'In the six hundredth year of Noah's life, in the second month, the seventeenth day of the month, the same day were all the fountains of the great deep broken up, and the windows of heaven were opened. And the rain was upon the earth forty days and forty nights' (Genesis 7:11-12). These verses are telling us that there was a cataclysmic disturbance in the earth beneath, and water comes up from below. And not only that, but also the canopy of water that was over the earth seems to have been removed. The windows of heaven were opened and the rain deluged down for forty days and forty nights. After the Flood the canopy is not there, but you have the climate as we know it, with the seasons, the rainfall and the sunshine. God pledges himself to them and gives Noah the assurance that these things will continue on through the running centuries (Genesis 8:22).

But there is a difference this side of the Flood from the other side of the Flood. Have you ever listened to any of these people protesting about nuclear power? They are always talking about radiation. They say that in the event of an accident the resulting radiation will adversely affect human beings. The lives of those who are immediately affected will be shortened, but succeeding generations will also be affected so that we cannot tell what will become of them. Physical mutations, so they argue, will occur for the worse. What do you think happened when that vast canopy of water vapour was removed from over the face of the earth—the canopy that shielded cosmic rays that otherwise would have come through the atmosphere and affected humanity? Remember, the removal of the canopy was part of the judgment of God that expressed itself in terms of the Flood. Is it not natural to suppose that it caused physical consequences in men's lives? Come to this side of the Flood, and when you begin to read of the length of men's lives you notice that they are much shorter. So we read in the Psalms: 'The days of our years are threescore years and ten; and if by reason of strength they be fourscore years, yet is their strength labour and sorrow; for it is soon cut off, and we fly away' (Psalm 90:10). Only in recent years, through the advances of medical science and environmental health, has the decline been arrested and reversed—although not returning to what it was in the early chapters of Scripture! Is not this a perfectly reasonable and rational explanation as to why it is possible to believe that in these early years men were living for this great period of time? But when the Flood came, everything was changed, relentlessly and with increasing rapidity. I am not suggesting that this is the only possible explanation, but to me it is a perfectly rational one. People inclined to dismiss these parts of Scripture as so much mythology and make-believe would do well to consider before they go on to mock them.

A man who pleased God

We would regard Enoch as an incredibly old man. Aged three hundred and sixty-five he does not die: God takes him away. In the language of the epistle to the Hebrews: 'By faith Enoch was translated that he should not see death; and was not found, because God had translated him: for before his translation he had this testimony, that he pleased God' (Hebrews 11:5). God comes to this man. God changes him. God removes him. That is what the word 'translation' actually means. He removes him from one state of existence to another. He takes him, in other words, from earth to heaven. You might argue that there is nothing unusual about that. It is something that happens in the case of every true believer in the Lord Jesus Christ. He or she is taken from earth to heaven. Yes, but in every other case, with the solitary exception of Elijah, it is via death. In the cases of Enoch and Elijah, neither died. Elijah was carried up on that chariot of fire. We are not given details of how it happened in the case of Enoch, and perhaps it is not profitable for us to speculate as to how he was changed without passing through death. He did not see death. God took him. He 'had this testimony, that he pleased God'.

Imagine God being able to say that of somebody! Do you not long that God should be able to say that of you? Think of all the fears that would be banished in a moment if you knew that such was God's testimony, God's witness-bearing, concerning you—'This man, this woman pleases me!' That was true of Enoch. He had this testimony, that he pleased God. Imagine the bewilderment of his family! Where is Enoch? He is gone. Did he die? No. Did he have an accident? No. What is the explanation? God has taken him. But has he not died like all the rest? In terms of the ages mentioned here he is a comparatively young man—barely coming up to what might have been described as middle-aged! But God took him because Enoch pleased him: 'for before his translation he had this testimony, that he pleased God'. This is the sort of man that we cannot just pass over, pretending that he is not in the Scriptures. God caused this account to be given of his life and of the testimony that God bore to him because there is obviously something tremendously important about this man Enoch. He walked with God. He pleased God.

In Hebrews 11:6 we are given what I would describe as a general principle that is expressed in the life and in the taking of Enoch: 'But without faith it is impossible to please him: for he that cometh to God must believe that he is, and that he is a rewarder of them that diligently seek him.'

What can we conclude from that about this man Enoch? It is this: Enoch had faith of such a calibre that it enabled him to walk with God. I do not think that we are meant to understand this in terms of walking with God physically—as though God somehow possessed a body and came down and walked with Enoch. But surely we are to understand it like this: there was communion between Enoch and God. He prayed. He knew God. He knew that when he prayed he was not talking to the air. Nor was he just projecting his thoughts in some psychological way, receiving a response that was produced by himself in the first place. No! He communed with God. It was something that he did habitually. It was not that once a week, at half past six on a Sunday night, he turned on a bit of religion, and sang a few hymns, and perhaps thought of some of the things he had heard about God. It was not that he met together with a few people who were likewise interested, and then in an hour or so went back home again until the following week! Enoch walked with God every day. Had you come across this man on any day of the week, you would have found him to be a godly man. He was not a man who prayed only in a crisis. He was a man to whom prayer was as natural as breathing. It was not that he sometimes wanted to please God. He *always* wanted to please God. Whatever he did, he did, as he saw it, to the glory and honour of God.

There is something very wonderful about a man of whom things like this can be said. He must have had faith in God, absolute faith that went out from himself to God and caused him, day by day, to walk in that habitual and lovely way with God. So it seems as if one day God, as it were, could restrain himself no longer and more or less said, 'I want this man in heaven.' And he took him there—translated him so that he should not see death. What a blessed and lovely end to his earthly life!

Some of the commentators on these early chapters of Scripture engage in what I believe to be some legitimate speculation. They say something like this. Could it have been that this is what God had in mind for Adam and Eve had they never sinned—indeed for the whole of humanity had they never sinned? It is not that they would just have gone on multiplying here upon earth so that earth would have become a very crowded planet. No! God, at the moment of his choosing, would have taken them to heaven —translated them so that they should not see death. This is speculation, of course. We cannot affirm it, and in a sense we cannot deny it, but to me it seems a perfectly reasonable speculation. In the case of Enoch it is not speculation; it is fact: 'By faith Enoch was translated that he should not see death . . . for before his translation he had this testimony, that he pleased God' (Hebrews 11:5).

The question that I want to put to you is a very simple one. What does God think of you? Is God pleased with you or is God angry with you? He certainly is not indifferent towards you. Is God pleased with you? We all know what it is, in ordinary human experience, to want some people to be pleased with us. Others we may not be concerned about. We do not mind treading on their toes and offending them, but we would think it a great tragedy if we caused some people to be displeased with us. The sad thing is that we, who understand this on a human level, so often forget all about it when we begin to think about God. Do I please God? Is he angry with me? Are the things that I do, the objects that I desire, the habits that I pursue, such as bring pleasure to God? Or are they such that they arouse his ire and anger? Think about it. What does God make of you? Is he pleased with you?

How we can please God

Here in the epistle to the Hebrews, the divinely inspired commentary on this little piece of history from the Old Testament, we are told how we can please God. Yes, we are told about Enoch:

> By faith Enoch was translated that he should not see death; and was not found, because God had translated him: for before his translation he had this testimony, that he pleased God. But without faith it is impossible to please him: for he that cometh to God must believe that he is, and that he is a rewarder of them that diligently seek him (Hebrews 11:5-6).

That is what Enoch believed. He believed that God is. You did not have to demonstrate the existence of God to Enoch. He knew that God is the living God, the only true and living God. God is! *You* know it in your hearts. Every man, even though he call himself an atheist, knows in his heart of hearts that there is a God. God made him. God has left the mark of his handiwork upon him so that he knows in his soul that there is a God. You too know that there is a God. In order that we may please God we need more than that sort of knowledge. We have to 'believe that he is, and that he is a rewarder of them that diligently seek him'. In other words, God never mocks those who pursue him. God is not some kind of tyrant, unfeeling, heartless, cruel, who invites men to come to him, but when they are seeking after him and calling upon him, turns round upon them and mocks them, saying, 'You fools. Did you think that I would listen to the likes of you?' God is not like that. God is honourable. God is the 'rewarder of them that diligently seek him'.

I do not know whether any intimation was ever given to

Enoch of what was going to happen to him. I do not suppose it really entered his imagination that one day this would happen—that God would somehow take him without causing him to pass through death. After all, he could look back to his ancestors and he could see that they had all died. Remember the seed of Seth, the line of Seth. That was the godly line. It was not like the rest of the world that was so corrupt and so deceitful—but even in the godly line all of them died. It must never have entered the imagination of Enoch that he would not die, but that he would be 'translated that he should not see death'. And yet he was seeking God, diligently seeking God, walking with God and pleasing God.

Does God matter to you, or is God something that you think about? I say 'something that you think about' deliberately. 'Something that you think about'—not the person that he is, not the God and Father of our Lord Jesus Christ who loved sinners and sent his Son into the world to die for them, but a kind of object, a thing. You might sing to him, you might argue about him, but he is almost impersonal and remote. What do you think of God? Do you ever seek him? Do you seek him in the way that is described here, not in a spasmodic, intermittent way, but do you *diligently* seek him?

As a minister of the gospel I have to deal from time to time with people who tell me they want to know God. Sometimes they are under considerable distress of soul, or so it seems to me. Then I see them perhaps a day or so later and it is all gone. There is no diligence, no wholehearted seeking after God. It was the passing emotion of a moment. That is not what is being spoken of here. 'He that cometh to God must believe that he is, and that he is a rewarder of them that diligently seek him' (Hebrews 11:6). Let me hold this before those of you who could truly say before God that you are seeking him and you long to know him. Seek him diligently and he will show himself to you. 'Seek,' said the Lord Jesus Christ, 'and ye shall find.' God does not mock. God leads you on that you might come to him and that you might find him.

Enoch and Elijah are unique. I am not preaching this sermon in order that I might hold before you, or before myself, the prospect that perhaps we shall not have to die. But I am preaching because I want to ask you, Do you seek God? Does he matter to you? Have you looked at your lives and asked whether they are pleasing to God? Do you have faith in the Lord Jesus Christ?

If you have faith in him, you do please God. All the beauty and perfection of Jesus is looked upon as belonging to you—even as all your vileness and sin are transferred to him. And God is pleased with you for the sake of Jesus Christ. Enoch was like that. He was born in sin as we all are. It was not that he had never sinned in his life. But through faith in God, in the promise of God, he pleased God, and in his sovereign mercy God came one day and took him on a walk that ended in heaven.

That is where Enoch is. Will you be there one day to join him? This is the way: 'But without faith it is impossible to please him: for he that cometh to God must believe that he is, and that he is a rewarder of them that diligently seek him.'

Chapter Four

When God's patience runs out

And the LORD *said, My spirit shall not*
always strive with man, for that he also is flesh: yet
his days shall be an hundred and twenty years.
(Genesis 6:3)

The early chapters of Genesis deal with issues of tremendous importance as far as the Word of God is concerned. The fact that the Lord Jesus Christ quoted from them on more than one occasion, as did the apostles, should be proof enough that these portions of Scripture matter. I emphasise the point because the spirit of the age tempts men and women to jettison these parts of the Word of God in particular. They may be willing to accept the Sermon on the Mount, as they think they can agree with it, or perhaps portions of the New Testament and the Psalms. But they draw back from these early parts of the Word of God in incredulity and unbelief, as if to say, 'That I cannot believe!' We must remember that the Lord Jesus Christ, the Son of God, the One without sin, whose knowledge was absolute, believed these passages.

For example, once when he was pleading with men and warning them, he reminded them in particular of events that are described in this and the next chapter. He was looking not just backwards but forward—forward to the end of the world, when he would return in glory, majesty and power. He speaks of a similarity between the state of mankind in the days of Noah and their state when he, the Lord Jesus Christ, will return the second time. He is quite explicit, speaking about marrying and giving in marriage, eating, drinking, doing all the things that human society does every day of every year. As it was then, he says, so shall it be in the day of the Son of Man. Look at that argument and you see it is very simple. Knock down the first half and you demolish the second. Some, in effect, say to the Lord, 'Did you not know what we know? Did you not know that there was no such man as Noah? Did you not know that there was no such thing as the Flood? Did you not know that the world was never destroyed?' Some audacious men reply to the Lord Jesus Christ like that! They may not spell it out in those exact words, but it is as if they say, 'We do not believe that you will come back the second time. We do not believe there is any truth or validity in your claims.'

I put it like this in order that you may see the issues starkly and plainly. If that is your view, you are setting yourself against the incarnate Son of God, the Lord Jesus Christ. He believed that these events happened, and he reasoned from them; and so did the apostles after him. We are not dealing here with realms of fantasy or fairy tale, with myth or saga, or anything like that! People think they can dignify it by using such a name and, by dignifying it, remove it from the realm of belief! We are not dealing with anything like that, but with what actually happened, in what I reckon is a historical progression.

We have considered that remarkable man Enoch, who walked with God and was taken by God, translated from this world to the eternal realm. God was pleased with him. He had faith in God and in God's promises. God took him from this world without taking him through the doorway of death, through which you and I will one day pass, barring the return of the Lord Jesus Christ. Two generations after Enoch we read of Lamech, who

> lived an hundred eighty and two years, and begat a son: and he called his name Noah, saying, This same shall comfort us concerning our work and toil of our hands, because of the ground which the LORD hath cursed. And Lamech lived after he begat Noah five hundred ninety and five years, and begat sons and daughters: and all the days of Lamech were seven hundred seventy and seven years: and he died. And Noah was five hundred years old: and Noah begat Shem, Ham, and Japheth (Genesis 5:28-32).

Unique and unparalleled

Then come the events of chapter 6. What Genesis does at this point is to give a general description of things upon earth at that time. It points us to something unparalleled in the whole of Scripture. There has been nothing else like the Flood and there never will be—until the Day of Judgment at the end of the world. Then it will not be flood but fire, and the holy wrath of Almighty God. Read on a few chapters, and you will discover that God himself has pledged that never again will he deal with the world in terms of a universal flood like that which he sent upon it and which is described for us in the next chapters. Here we are dealing with something that is unique and unparalleled. There is nothing you can turn to which casts any light upon it; it stands absolutely on its own. It is as if, putting it in merely human terms, things became so bad that God was driven to do something terrible and devastating.

That, I think, is the picture these verses give us.

The chapter begins with the intermingling of the sons of God and the daughters of men. I think we are to understand these as being two lines of descendants from Adam—the line originated by Cain, described largely in Genesis 4, and the other line, the godly line of Seth, described in Genesis 5. It seems that they were separate from one another, having nothing in common apart from their humanity. The line that traced its ancestry back to Cain lived in the light of that ancestry. Any godliness to be found on the earth was found in the other line, namely that descending from Seth. Genesis 5 brings the genealogy of Seth's descendants right down to Noah and his family.

The picture that follows is one of increasing deterioration, increasing turning away from God. We find that the two lines are now intermingling, so that even the godliness of the one line is in danger of being snuffed out. At that point we have these words: 'And the LORD said, My spirit shall not always strive with man, for that he also is flesh: yet his days shall be an hundred and twenty years' (Genesis 6:3). God is issuing a threat. He is saying that things have come to such a pass that his patience is almost exhausted. There will be a hundred and twenty years and then, as far as this generation is concerned, the end will come. 'I will stop striving with men and I will stop the Holy Spirit coming to plead with men to restrain and reason with them. My spirit shall not always strive with man.' Men had become just like flesh—animals—they were so corrupt and debased. Yet God says, 'I am still going to give them one hundred and twenty years.'

A preacher of righteousness
During those one hundred and twenty years Noah, who is

to be central in the next few chapters, preached. He preached and built an ark. Peter, in his second epistle, called Noah a 'preacher of righteousness' (2 Peter 2:5). You have to admire this man, living probably in the middle of Mesopotamia, far from the sea, and building this enormous boat. Its actual dimensions are given to us later on: it was three hundred cubits long, fifty cubits wide and fifty cubits high (450 x 75 x 75 feet), with three decks. It was an enormous boat. Some modern-day naval architects have commented on the capaciousness of the vessel and its suitability for the purpose for which it was designed.

Noah and his small family are building this ark. People come to laugh at him. You can understand it. Have you seen anybody building such an enormous boat so far from the sea? You can predict the sort of jokes they would have cracked at Noah's expense: 'Where are you going to launch it, Noah? Who will be the captain?' and so on. He must have been the laughing stock of the country. Noah would have preached and told them why he was building the ark. God was going to send a terrible flood, a flood that would annihilate the whole of mankind, apart from those who would be safe and secure in this vessel that he was building. And God had commanded him to bring various animals of all sorts into the ark.

Over this long period of time Noah was constructing the ark. His contemporaries must have thought it the height of folly. Yet he went on as a preacher of righteousness, warning of the impending judgment of God. Evidently nobody, apart from members of his family, believed him. When the time came for Noah to enter the ark, only they go in with him; the rest are outside. The Lord *shut Noah in*—that is what this book of Genesis says. The rest of mankind received the judgment of God. It was a terrible judgment—

one that was not only predicted but that actually fell upon the whole earth. What caused God to take that unprecedented and unparalleled step? What brought him to the extreme of judging the world like this—of saying in effect, 'My patience is exhausted; the Holy Spirit is no longer going to strive with men'?

The first half of Genesis 6 tells us in detail what things were like. For example: 'And GOD saw that the wickedness of man was great in the earth . . . And it repented the LORD that he had made man on the earth, and it grieved him at his heart' (Genesis 6:5-6). That describes God in human language that we can understand; but such human emotions do not really apply to him. God, unlike us, never needs to repent. He never needs to change his mind. His purposes are settled from eternity. He never needs second thoughts or to adjust his plans. Here he is spoken of as if he were human. (The technical term for this is 'anthropomorphism'.) He is spoken of in this way so that we might be able to understand something of what God was doing. God *saw* the terrible wickedness. It was so great that 'every imagination of the thoughts of [man's] heart was only evil continually' (Genesis 6:5). These words are not describing trivial conditions of sin. Sin was rampant; sin had conquered man in every power and every faculty. There was such terrible wickedness in the earth that God said, 'I repent of ever having made man. I am going to bring to an end all men except Noah and those of his family who believe in me.'

An ungodly society

We are also told: 'The earth also was corrupt before God . . . and, behold, I will destroy them with the earth' (Genesis 6:11,13). This is a picture of an ungodly society, a corrupt and evil society, one that has become so profoundly wicked that God is driven to the point of destroying it. And not only was there moral corruption in men's thoughts and lives, but violence as well. Terrible violence had broken out upon the earth. We saw this in a previous chapter when we considered Lamech (not the Lamech who was Noah's father, but one of the descendants of Cain): 'And Lamech said unto his wives, Adah and Zillah . . . I have slain a man to my wounding, and a young man to my hurt. If Cain shall be avenged sevenfold, truly Lamech seventy and sevenfold' (Genesis 4:23-24).

The Authorised Version translates Genesis 6:4 as 'There were giants in the earth in those days'. The word is *nephilim*. We are not altogether sure of its meaning, but it refers to men with great physical powers. Hundreds of years later, when the children of Israel were going to the Promised Land, they sent twelve spies ahead. Ten returned saying that the land was beautiful and wonderful, everything they had been led to expect—but there were *giants* in the land, and so they would never be able to conquer it (Numbers 13:33). This is the same word as is used here in Genesis 6:4. It seems to indicate men of great physical strength and prowess. They are actually called 'men of renown'.

This, then, was the state of antediluvian society at the time of Noah. There was great wickedness, evil imagination, moral corruption and awful violence. They all go together, don't they? How up to date this old book is! Here is something that could almost be a reflection of Britain today. Moral corruption? Can you turn on your television and watch a drama or a comedy programme without running the risk of corrupting yourself? You know that it is very likely that all life's sanctities will be trampled underfoot, with marriage held up to ridicule and immorality shown as the 'in thing' that everyone practises. Violence? Open the pages of any newspaper and you have the answer to that! In recent years there have been so many instances of brutality and violence. But does not that just highlight the nature of our society? We now witness violence in many areas where at one time it was not to be found. In what are supposedly friendly sports, supporters or players of one side resort to violence against the other side. This is just a reflection of our society. Whole areas of our towns and cities are no longer safe for people, particularly women; they fear to walk at night because they do not know what might happen. We have almost a re-enacting of the state of affairs that obtained before God sent the Flood on the earth. People tell you that this book is outdated, but they do not know what they are talking about! The Scriptures are the most up-to-date and relevant commentary on the state of affairs in our land, and they explain it as well.

Why had things come to this terrible pass? Go right back to Genesis 3, and that original sin in the Garden of Eden. The seed of sin has been planted into the heart of every man and woman born into this world, with the solitary exception of the Lord Jesus Christ. Then, in Genesis 4, you see men deliberately setting themselves against God, shaking their fists in his face, regarding his threats as empty threats, and going on in the way of ungodliness. So you get this outbreak of violence; you get immorality, lust—unbridled lust seems to break forth. It is all here, just as it is in our society today. But in this sixth chapter God says, 'Thus far and no farther. I cannot allow it to go beyond this.' God is provoked to act.

The godly line
God began taking action when even the godly line of Seth

became corrupted. Hitherto there were two lines, one godly, the other ungodly. The line of Cain was characterised by ungodliness, and the line of Seth had a semblance (and in many cases more than that) of true godliness. But what happened? 'And it came to pass . . . they took them wives of all which they chose' (Genesis 6:1-2). Here then was something new. There had not been intermarrying before, so a godly line had been preserved. It would have been an unheard-of thing for a daughter or a son of this godly line to intermarry with those ungodly people; such a thing had not happened. But suddenly we find in chapter 6 that it is happening. Standards have gone. No longer is there a line that will be preserved in its godliness. The evil from without is coming in and corrupting the line of Seth. That is the last straw, as it were, as far as God is concerned.

Let us pause for a moment. Here is the first of a not inconsiderable number of scriptural references to the fact that the godly ought not to marry the ungodly. There is a verse in 2 Corinthians that is often used in this context to express the general principle. The apostle Paul says: 'Be ye not unequally yoked together with unbelievers: for what fellowship hath righteousness with unrighteousness? and what communion hath light with darkness?' (2 Corinthians 6:14). This statement does apply to marriage, of course, though not only to marriage. If you are a Christian and, quite naturally, you are wanting in the providence of God to be married, do not contemplate marriage to someone who does not share your faith in the Lord Jesus Christ. This is a principle running right through Scripture. What you will be doing—barring the special grace of God, on which we must not presume, although sometimes he exercises it in the most amazing way—is setting yourself up to be pulled down by your partner. You will not pull your spouse up. As a minister of the gospel I have seen this happen many, many times. Here is the beginning of that principle. What a terrible beginning it is, when these two lines intermingle and God says, 'That's enough. Things have gone too far'! As far as the world is concerned God's judgment is but a foregone conclusion. That is what this chapter describes to us—and it is a quite contemporary situation as far as we are concerned.

Striving with men

I want to call your attention to what God says at this point: 'And the LORD said, My spirit shall not always strive with man' (Genesis 6:3). What God had been doing so far was striving with men: pleading with them, restraining them, urging them to obey what was right, good and true. He had done this from the time of Adam and Eve in the Garden of Eden and through succeeding generations. He had not left himself without a witness; he had striven by the Holy Spirit with men. This is hinted at in chapters 4 and 5.

Can I put it like this? God's purposes and God's grace succeed.

> And Adam knew his wife again; and she bare a son, and called his name Seth: For God, said she, hath appointed me another seed instead of Abel, whom Cain slew. And to Seth, to him also there was born a son; and he called his name Enos: then began men to call upon the name of the LORD (Genesis 4:25-26).

Into a degenerate and corrupt society comes a glimmer of light. Men begin to call upon the name of the Lord. A prayer meeting, a service, a little gathering of the faithful in the line descended from Seth: 'then began men to call upon the name of the LORD'.

Remember Enoch, whom we considered in the previous chapter, or even Lamech, the father of Noah. The latter was a man of faith, and when Noah was born he spoke of him saying: 'This same shall comfort us [the name Noah means 'rest' or 'comfort'] concerning our work and toil of our hands, because of the ground which the LORD hath cursed' (Genesis 5:29). Lamech had the conviction that God would use this son for blessing, and he expresses faith and hope in God.

Generally speaking, however, such things were conspicuous by their absence. Increasing deterioration, terrible moral and spiritual degeneration, is all too apparent. Inevitably, when men turn from God, society deteriorates. It has to do so. When God is disowned, sooner or later everything will decay. The values and principles taken for granted before are first questioned, and then rejected.

It is now more than thirty years since the passing of the Abortion Act. Who would have thought twenty-five years ago that millions of babies would have been slaughtered in our land? Not by some monster of a tyrant in some other country, of whom we could say, 'You can understand him doing it—after all, he was Adolf Hitler!', but by people in Britain, so-called 'Christian' Britain! Who would have thought that it would have come to that? But it goes on from that. If you are not too careful about preserving life in the womb, what about the child born with a deformity or abnormality? Some medical people argue that it would be kinder just to snuff out its life. That has undoubtedly happened in some places. Project it on to the other end of life, the end to which we all move relentlessly and inevitably. Euthanasia is now put forward as a perfectly reasonable, civilised way of slipping out of time—not into eternity because they do not believe in that—and of writing the end of the chapter of our human existence. Twenty-five years ago such things were deemed impossible in Britain! Yet perfectly intelligent, rational people are advocating these things today. Who knows if in our own lifetime some of these unthinkable things will be made legal and regarded as normal in our society? Do not believe those saying that society does not change! It does. When a society turns away from God we do not know what its end point will be.

Here we see one of the many instances in the Word of God of a society that has turned from God—turned towards lust and immorality and violence and crime—ultimately coming under the judgment of God. It is inevitable. That is the story we read here. Into the situation God speaks this last word of warning. 'My patience is almost exhausted, my grace has almost reached to its ultimate limit', he is saying. 'My spirit shall not always strive with man, for that he also is flesh: yet his days shall be an hundred and twenty years' (Genesis 6:3).

The grace of God

A hundred and twenty years—then judgment! That is the situation described here. And this is a principle not to be missed. God's grace is a marvellous thing, but it is not to be presumed upon. God is long-suffering and merciful; many texts in the Scriptures tell us this. Where would any of us be, were it not for God's long-suffering and mercy? The first time we sinned God could have snuffed us out in judgment and we would have had no complaint! But he did not do it. He is merciful, patient, and long-suffering. He gives men and women space and time to repent, even when they sin again and again, as all of us have done. We have broken promises before God and have committed sins of all kinds; but still God holds back his hand. He strives with us, pleads with us, reasons with us. Thank God, we can see the result of God's patience in some old lag who, after a life of wickedness, turns to the Lord Jesus Christ, passes from death to life and goes to heaven when he dies. It is a great blessing to remember that conversions do take place late in life; but there is a danger that men *presume* upon the grace of God.

There are many reasons why they do so. We can imagine how men must have reasoned in Noah's day. Did they ask this question: 'Who needs God; or who needs that God of Noah? So precise, so particular, telling you what to do and what not to do! Always making us feel uncomfortable with the things we do and say and think! Who wants that sort of God?' So they rejected him. Chapter 4 shows that here was no primitive civilisation but a highly developed one, with the arts, music, and culture. There was also great prosperity and the beginnings of industry. Everything seemed to be going on marvellously—mankind developing, cities being built, riches gathered in. Also there was this fantastic life span—not threescore and ten or fourscore years, but seven or eight or, in some cases, nine hundred years before men died. Death seemed banished to a very distant future. That was how men reasoned. 'Here we are, rich and prosperous; we have never had it so good! It's not just that we have money, but we also have these cultural enjoyments and amusements—marvellous music and the rest of it. It is great when we have our carousing and our enjoyment; we are able to experience beautiful things! If there really is a God, if he really means what he says about sin and judgment, why hasn't he come and judged us? Why hasn't he struck us down the moment we sinned?' They reason that perhaps he is not there; or if he is, he is not as precise as preachers like Noah claim. 'We can ignore him,' they say. 'In any case we have hundred of years left yet. Perhaps nearer the time we will think of these things.'

What they were doing was presuming upon the grace of God. Is that not what some of you are doing? You do not work in their timescale of seven, eight or nine hundred years, but you reason in the identical way. 'That preacher! Always on about sin! Always on about death and judgment! I have lived a long time—nothing like that has happened to me yet. This is a fairy story!' Can you imagine these people? They would probably meet and say, 'What do you think about Adam and Eve? Do you believe all that they say went on in the Garden of Eden? Do you believe God came down and put cherubim with a flaming sword barring entrance into the Garden? The tree of life, the forbidden fruit and all the rest of it—do you really believe that fairy tale?' I expect men reasoned in that way then, just as some of you reason in that way now. If you do, you are presuming upon the grace of God. God is giving you space to repent, and you seem to be saying, 'God, don't bother! In any case I won't repent. I'm not interested in that sort of thing. I may be in the house of God now, by constraint, or out of habit or respect for somebody else—but this is not for me!' God warns you, and this is what he says: 'My spirit shall not always strive with man'.

God is not obliged to strive with you. Why should he? You heard the gospel once and rejected it. Why should God bother a second time? Millions in this world have never heard of Jesus Christ, let alone had the gospel preached to them. Why should God bother with you when you have heard it at least once—and may have heard it hundreds of times?

Why resist God? God comes, and he strives through the preaching of the Word. God strives with that great ally in your own soul, your conscience. You know it; it is an awkward thing to have. At times we wish we had no conscience, but we cannot get rid of it. It reasons with us: 'You ought not to have done that. It is wrong, you know. You will regret it!' We stifle it; we try to silence it; we try to diminish its influence—but it goes on and on. It can be the voice of God speaking, restraining us, pulling us back, and giving us space to repent. The voice of conscience may sometimes be as mundane as the restraints of even a corrupt society; or family restraints keeping us from the extremes to which we might go. It is one way in which God comes and strives with sinners. Or perhaps a Christian speaks to you about your soul and the Saviour, your sin and your need of salvation. And you find it so irksome; you wish he would shut up, go home and leave you alone! But God is striving with you and saying, 'I'm not always going to plead with you. Why should I?' The time comes when there is a cut-off point in the grace and the mercy of God.

Our Lord Jesus Christ knew that this is so. On the brow of the hill overlooking Jerusalem, he wept because he knew that for its people the day of grace was over. Its inhabitants had rejected him. All that lay in store for them now was the judgment of God. It fell upon their city less than forty years after the Lord Jesus Christ's death. Jesus said: 'O Jerusalem, Jerusalem . . . how often would I have gathered thy children together, as a hen doth gather her brood under her wings, and ye would not!' (Luke 13:34). 'My spirit shall not always strive with man' was as true then as it was in the time of Noah.

A way of escape

God, dear friend, may well be striving with you. You are troubled in your conscience. You sense that God is speaking to you about your sin. God's day of mercy, God's day of grace up to this moment has not ended. But there may be no more moments of grace for you. Do not presume that there will be. Are you going to yield and believe on the Lord Jesus Christ? Will you recognise the corruption and sinfulness of your heart, and the holiness of the living God, with whom one day you will have to do? Or do you put your fingers in your ears and dismiss it as complete nonsense? Will you stifle your conscience, reject parental restraint and that of society about you? Will you deny the truth of the Word of God and rush down the road leading inevitably to hell? The choice is yours. God says, 'My spirit shall not always strive with man'.

But now as you read these words he does strive, he does plead. He sets before you his Son, the Lord Jesus Christ, and he offers you, in the midst of a corrupt, wicked and adulterous generation, a way of escape. He offers you peace with himself, pardon for sin, reconciliation with God, and a home in heaven when you die. He sets all these blessings before you, and he says that if you but turn to the Lord Jesus Christ, all these, and more, will be yours. He pleads, he strives by his Holy Spirit with you!

What will you do? Will you go the way of those poor damned sinners that laughed at the 'preacher of righteousness' and throughout eternity have regretted every occasion that they scorned God and his offers of grace? They found out too late that there is no way that leads from hell to heaven. Will that be your story? Or will you come to Jesus Christ and believe upon him?

Chapter Five
What is man?

*And God blessed Noah and his sons,
and said unto them, Be fruitful, and multiply,
and replenish the earth. And the fear of you and the
dread of you shall be upon every beast of the earth,
and upon every fowl of the air, upon all that moveth
upon the earth, and upon all the fishes of the sea;
into your hand are they delivered. Every moving
thing that liveth shall be meat for you; even as the
green herb have I given you all things. But flesh with
the life thereof, which is the blood thereof, shall ye
not eat. And surely your blood of your lives will I
require; at the hand of every beast will I require it,
and at the hand of man; at the hand of every man's
brother will I require the life of man. Whoso sheddeth
man's blood, by man shall his blood be shed:
for in the image of God made he man.*
(Genesis 9:1-6)

The words recorded for us in these verses come after the Flood, that amazing display of the judgment of God on an exceedingly sinful world. The Flood had subsided and the ark came down to rest on Mount Ararat. Noah found himself able to release the animals he had gathered into the ark, and eventually Noah, his wife, his sons and daughters-in-law left the ark. They began to remake their life upon the earth, which in many ways was a new earth, purged of the corrupt and wicked race that had perished in the Flood. Just this one family was preserved, a family that took God at his word, a family that believed the threats and warnings of God, and that was delivered by trusting in God's promise.

This is really a totally new situation. But as you read on in this same chapter, you see that in many ways it is the same old world all over again. Sin had not been eradicated from this family, nor even from this man Noah, who stood head and shoulders above the rest of the world, and whose faith in God and fearless proclamation of the word of God had marked him out from his contemporaries. The chapter ends on a very sad note, with Noah getting drunk and lying indecently exposed in his tent. The whole sad story of man's sin seems to be starting all over again.

But here at the end of the eighth and the beginning of the ninth chapters we have an account of Noah and his family leaving the ark, and of God speaking to Noah and entering into a covenant with him. Noah had taken extra numbers of clean (as opposed to unclean) animals into the ark, obviously for the purpose of sacrifice. Now, on leaving the ark, he offers a sacrifice of some of those clean animals. It is a sacrifice of thanksgiving to God, and God is pleased to accept it.

And Noah builded an altar unto the LORD; and took of every clean beast, and of every clean fowl, and offered burnt offerings on the altar. And the LORD smelled a sweet savour; and the LORD said in his heart, I will not again curse the ground any more for man's sake; for the imagination of man's heart is evil from his youth; neither will I again smite any more every thing living, as I have done. While the earth remaineth, seedtime and harvest, and cold and heat, and summer and winter, and day and night shall not cease (Genesis 8:20-22).

A new beginning

It seems to be a new start, a start which echoes the beginning described in Genesis 1. For example, the commandment God gave Adam and Eve in the Garden of Eden is reiterated. Of Adam and Eve we read: 'And God blessed them, and God said unto them, Be fruitful, and multiply, and replenish the earth, and subdue it' (Genesis 1:28). God now says the same thing to Noah and his sons: 'And God blessed Noah and his sons, and said unto them, Be fruitful, and multiply, and replenish the earth' (Genesis 9:1).

It seems reasonable to conclude that before the Flood man had been a vegetarian, eating only the plants God had placed on the earth. But now God says that it is perfectly legitimate for him to eat animals as well. Certain restrictions are to be enforced later in the Old Testament, but here there is but one restriction: he must not eat animal blood. 'But flesh with the life thereof, which is the blood thereof, shall ye not eat.' Scripture says that blood is a symbol of the life of the animal, and that before the flesh is eaten the blood of the animal must be drained off from it. This restriction is observed by the Jews to this day.

Then, no doubt reflecting on what things were like before the Flood, God brings in something new. He mentions murder, and retribution for the crime of murder. 'Whoso sheddeth man's blood, by man shall his blood be shed: for in the image of God made he man' (Genesis 9:6).

What were things like before the Flood? In the sixth chapter of Genesis we read: 'The earth also was corrupt before God, and the earth was filled with violence' (Genesis 6:11). In Genesis 4 we have the first murder: Cain murders his brother Abel. At the end of that chapter we meet a man called Lamech: 'And Lamech said unto his wives, Adah and Zillah, Hear my voice; ye wives of Lamech, hearken unto my speech: for I have slain a man to my wounding, and a young man to my hurt' (Genesis 4:23). He boasts of his violence in a little ditty: 'I am mighty! I am powerful! I have killed a man! Who can do anything to me by way of retribution?' Things began like that, and they deteriorated. By the time God had determined to visit the world with the Flood, it had become a place of great corruption and exceeding violence. Life was cheap; there was no legal process for vengeance, and no justice for those guilty of violent crime, particularly murder.

Now, on this side of the Flood, God makes provision for that. He does so even in the case of animals. An animal that attacks and kills a man is to be destroyed. Likewise the life of a murderer is to be forfeit. 'And surely your blood of your lives will I require; at the hand of every beast will I require it, and at the hand of man; at the hand of every man's brother will I require the life of man' (Genesis 9:5). God here emphasises the sanctity of life, which occupies an important, indeed a prominent, position in the unfolding story of revelation. Few things in our modern world are more relevant than what God says here about man, his nature, the value of his life, and what is to happen when a man takes away another man's life by cold premeditated murder. I want to emphasise the reason behind the penalty more that the penalty itself. Notice how verse 6 puts it: 'Whoso sheddeth man's blood, by man shall his blood be shed'. Why? God immediately gives the answer: 'for in the image of God made he man'.

The image of God
The same phrase occurs back in Genesis 1: 'And God said, Let us make man in our image, after our likeness . . . So God created man in his own image, in the image of God created

he him; male and female created he them' (Genesis 1:26-27). When God created man, he made him in his image and likeness. What does this mean? It does not mean what we normally mean by an image: that is, a statue, a likeness, a representation of some human being. Perhaps you have been to a museum and art gallery and have admired statues made by great sculptors and have seen the likeness of a famous personality captured in the material the sculptor has been working in. God is not speaking of that when he speaks of the image of God being there in man. It is simple to prove that. God is Spirit; he has no body. You cannot take God and make a likeness of him in the material sense. Jesus said: 'God is a Spirit: and they that worship him must worship him in spirit and in truth' (John 4:24). So all statues, all images, are ruled out in the worship of God, because the invisible, spiritual God cannot be put into a human likeness. It is not just inappropriate; it is utterly and absolutely wrong; the two are incompatible. The image of God does not mean a physical replica.

When God made man in his image, it is not as if he looked at himself, and then began to fashion man: two arms, two legs, a head, a trunk, fingers and toes and the rest. It is something more profound than that, something far more significant—it is something spiritual. Let me put it like this. When people have tried to understand what is meant by the image of God, the most satisfactory explanation that is scriptural runs along these lines.

In response to the question What is man? the answer is, in the first place, that man is a *rational* being. That does not mean that he is hyper-intelligent. When we speak of man as a rational being we are not speaking of degrees of intelligence; rather we are saying that he has this faculty, this power of reasoning. Sometimes we may wonder if we have this at all because we make terrible mistakes! Yet isn't this one of the things that marks us off from the animals—this power, this faculty of being able to think and reason? The zoologists tell us that chimpanzees, which you may smile at when you see them in television adverts, are supposed to be the highest in the animal realm. And if they are trained for years they can be made to do simple things in order to receive two bananas! But that is not rationality in the sense that you and I are rational, intelligent beings.

The image of God in man means not only that he is a rational being. It means also that man is a *moral* being. God made Adam and Eve and put them in the Garden of Eden under ideal conditions, but he put a moral restraint on them. There were things that they could and ought to do, but there was something that they were not to do: they were not to eat the fruit of the forbidden tree. That injunction stood as something of a moral test. Man is a moral being. He is able to understand morality. He knows what is right and what is wrong. He understands the difference between right and wrong. Man made in the image of God is made with this capacity to understand the area of morality. He knows he is under an obligation to obey God.

Add to these a third thing and you begin to reach a more complete understanding of what is meant by the image of God. Man is not only a rational being and a moral being, but he is also a *spiritual* being. Man was made to worship God. You have this in the first two chapters of Genesis. It is as if God were in the habit of coming down in a wonderful, spiritual, mysterious way and communing with Adam. Adam was made to worship God. Augustine, one of the great fathers of the Christian Church who lived in about AD 400, put it like this: ' Thou hast made us for Thyself, and our hearts are restless until they find their rest in Thee.'

God has implanted in your heart and mine, and in the heart of every human being, a need for him—a need to worship him, to fall down before him and worship him as God.

The image debased

In Adam and Eve before the Fall the image of God was there in its perfection. There was nothing to mar it, nothing to spoil it, nothing to detract from it. The image of God in perfection characterised them. It is not like that now! The third chapter of Genesis shows us why this is so. It tells us of the Fall of man, of man's rebellion against God, of man shaking his fist in the face of God and saying defiantly, 'I am not going to do what you tell me! I am going to do what I want to do!' Noah's contemporaries stand on this side of the Fall. They still have the image of God in them. They are still rational; they still have this moral capacity; they still have this spirituality by which they need to worship God. But something has happened to the image of God. It has become marred, twisted, spoiled and debased, but it is still there!

So when God speaks this verse to Noah, as he is beginning life all over again after the Flood, he says to him: 'Whoso sheddeth man's blood, by man shall his blood be shed'. Then he gives the reason: 'for in the image of God made he man'. That, God says, is why violence against another human being is an evil thing—so evil that it even calls for the vengeance of God, so that the guilty man must pay with his life.

In Britain today, and in many other countries, there is no death penalty. Those old enough to remember the arguments leading first to the suspension and then to the abolition of the death penalty will remember that its abolition was looked upon as a great advance. If you said to the formers of moral opinion in this country, 'Look, he has committed a heinous crime and he ought to pay with his life', they would say, 'Don't be old-fashioned! That is mere retribution. That barbarism does not belong to the twentieth century!' One is tempted to ask, Have murders decreased? Have crimes of violence disappeared? On the contrary, life has been cheapened, which was an entirely predictable consequence.

When God gives this commandment which demands that a man's life be forfeit if he takes another man's life, we are not talking about war; we are thinking in terms of murder. God is saying that a man's life is a precious thing—precious because his image is in man. If you assault another man, you are really assaulting the living God, because that man is the image-bearer of God. Therefore, God says that justice demands that the death penalty be carried out against the perpetrator of murder.

When the arguments for the abolition of the death penalty were being advanced, it was claimed that people would have an enhanced view of life if it were held to be so valuable that even the life of a murderer could not be taken. It was predictable that people would say, 'I will do it. They will only put me in prison—perhaps for a long time—but they are not going to execute me for my crime!' So life has been cheapened, because legislators have thought that they could fly in the face of what God has said and yet somehow elevate the status of life. No! God is wise. God knows what he is doing. Our society, in breaking this commandment that God has given, does so to its own sorrow and suffering.

Another argument advanced by those advocating the abolition of the death penalty was that two hundred years ago there were about two hundred offences for which a man could be hanged. A poor man caught sheep-stealing could be hanged for it. People said, 'Look at that! You surely do not hang a man for that!' Of course they were right; hanging was an inappropriate penalty for theft. But they went on to argue that the death penalty itself was wrong. God says no! Man's life is precious because he is the image-bearer of God, and when a man murders another, by man shall his own blood be shed!

That is not a counsel of despair. In the great Methodist Revival two hundred and fifty years ago, John and Charles Wesley and many other less famous men would go into the prisons and to the places of execution. They would minister to prisoners awaiting execution, and time and time again such were converted and brought into the kingdom of God before they died. They were brought to realise the awfulness of the crimes they had committed, and before they paid the penalty as far as their bodies were concerned, their souls were reconciled to God, they were at peace with him and ready to die. There are stirring accounts of one or other of the Wesley brothers, on the cart going to Tyburn or some other place of execution, preaching, praying and singing hymns with prisoners who were on their way to their death. Around them were people like some mob going to a football match. And here were men going home to glory, men who in some cases had been murderers, and yet the blood of Jesus Christ had washed away their sins. That is simply a fact of history.

God's special creation

I do not want to major on the death penalty. I mention it because it is so clearly in the text, setting before us what we could call the 'dignity of man'. Man is God's special creation. Genesis 1 comes to its climax with an account of how God created man as the summit of his creation. God created the world. The sun, the stars, the moon and the planets are all placed there in the heavens. The earth is created, the sea is created, the vegetation on earth is created, the animals are created. But man does not come from any of these. Man is created separately and specially by God. In Genesis 1 we read: 'and let them have dominion over the fish of the sea, and over the fowl of the air, and over the cattle, and over all the earth, and over every creeping thing that creepeth upon the earth' (Genesis 1:26). Man is to have dominion over everything else that has been created. Man was made as the crown and summit of God's creation. He was made for this special place of dignity.

This is one reason why the theory of evolution (and remember that it is at best a theory!) is such a pernicious thing. It says to man, 'Ultimately there is nothing special about you as a man. You are a highly developed animal. You are not the result of God's special creation. You are here by some mysterious process of evolution from the animal kingdom which can be traced back to some primeval lump of sludge.' How the inanimate became animate, or how life came in the place of death, they do not know, they cannot answer. They put it all forth as dogma.

So runs the theory of evolution that has taken possession of so much of modern thinking. It has become not just a theory of man's physical origins but a theory of the development of history and the process of civilisation. Man is improving; man is getting better. He has come up from something primitive and inanimate and is improving all the time. You would have thought that stark facts would have stopped all such nonsense. Is it a coincidence that since the publication of Darwin's *Origin of Species* and its acceptance by the so-called intelligentsia, we have had such terrible world wars, such devastation, such widespread death and suffering? Men getting better and better? It does not make sense. Is man better now than in Bible times? Is he nobler? I know that in one sense his intellect seems to have developed, in that he is able to do things he could not do formerly. He has made all sorts of scientific discoveries, but is he any better morally? Is he higher than these people in the early chapters of Genesis, when there was this great corruption and terrible violence upon earth? If you want to identify Britain with any place in the Bible today, I suggest that it is here in Genesis or in Romans chapter 1. Man is not getting better and better; instead, he seems to be hopelessly in the grip of his own weakness, sin and failure.

Is not this one of the great arguments against the theory of evolution? Tell a man that he is an animal, and it is predictable that he will behave like one. Why shouldn't he, if that is all he is? If he is just a rather intelligent animal, a 'naked ape' as Desmond Morris has called him, why should he not behave as animals do? So many people in our society are doing just that. They have no morals; they are totally immoral. They are in fact amoral, without any moral values at all. They have no religion; there is no worship of God. They are anti-God, they scorn God, they despise God.

It is remarkable to note the way in which modern man has taken each of these three aspects of the image of God and reversed them. Man made in the image of God is a *rational* creature. What do you find in modern thinking and culture? Irrationality, the absence of reason. Have you ever stood before some of these works of modern art and asked what they mean? If you ask, What is the artist trying to say, and how does that fit in with man as a rational human being? the answer that comes back is that irrationality has taken the place of reason.

And then *morality*—for man is a moral creature. In the

last ten, twenty, thirty years we have seen the outbreak not simply of immorality but of amorality. People used to have a sense of guilt in their hearts when they did wrong—but not now! Why should they obey God? Why should they be what some call moral? Why should they be faithful to their marriage partner? Why shouldn't they tell lies and be greedy? Who is to say what is right and what is wrong? Amorality!

Then when it comes to the *spiritual* aspect of man, it is not just a matter of ignoring God. There is a spirit of anti-God—people hating God, wanting to put the knife into a Christian and twist it whenever they get the opportunity. You do not get a fair hearing on the media; instead, this anti-God spirit seems to pervade the age. Man has turned away from God, and although he has been made in the image of God, he is trying to place a veil over that image. It is a marred, a fallen, a spoiled image; but it is still recognisably the image of God.

Have you ever asked the question, Why is it that racial prejudice is wrong? Why is it wrong to discriminate against somebody on the basis of his colour? It happens in different ways in different parts of the world. It is not always white against black; it may be the other way round and all sorts in between. The only adequate explanation as to why it is wrong is that, whatever a person's colour, that person is made in the image of God. What people are doing is, in effect, discriminating against God, because the person they are discriminating against is someone bearing God's image.

Why is abortion wrong, except in perhaps the most extenuating circumstances? It is wrong because that embryonic child in the womb of the mother bears the image of God. So, for women to talk of rights over their own bodies as if that is all that had to be taken into account is wrong.

The unborn child they are carrying is not a non-person, not just a collection of cells; that child is made in God's image. To ignore this truth is totally to misunderstand the situation.

The same arguments apply in the realms of justice and morality. Why should there be justice and fairness in men's dealings with one another? This is ultimately because we are made in the image of God. We stand neither above nor below one another. There may be minor distinctions, but looked at from this perspective all such distinctions fade to obscurity and insignificance. All of us bear the image of God. That is what the Lord is saying to Noah: 'Whoso sheddeth man's blood, by man shall his blood be shed: for in the image of God made he man' (Genesis 9:6).

What is man?
The fundamental question we have to ask is this. What is man? What are you? What am I? Have you ever thought of this question? How would you describe a man? I am not thinking in physical terms, of weight, height, colour, and the rest of it. But what essentially *is* man? What is it that is different about man? This is something the so-called humanists have no answer for. (The title 'humanist' is totally inappropriate because humanists, above everybody else, debase and belittle man. They do not recognise him as somebody made by and for God.)

Man is a great paradox in many ways. He is capable of such marvellous achievements. We live in a century unsurpassed for its scientific advances and discoveries. Nowadays we take for granted things previously undreamed of even in the realm of science fiction. Who knows what will be happening in ten, twenty, thirty years' time if advances continue as they have been doing in the scientific realm? Man is capable of almost limitless achievement. A man may be capable of producing great music and literature that can move and satisfy you. And yet that same person may live his life as if he is scarcely removed from the animals. Indeed in some cases the animals seem to have more morality than such individuals!

What is man? He is a terrible enigma. Shakespeare expressed it in one of Hamlet's soliloquies:

> What a piece of work is man! How noble in reason! how infinite in faculties! in form and moving, how express and admirable! in action, how like an angel! in apprehension, how like a god! the beauty of the world! the paragon of animals! And yet, to me, what is this quintessence of dust? (*Hamlet* II. ii.)

So exalted, but what is he?—'this quintessence of dust'—'dust thou art, and unto dust shalt thou return' (Genesis 3:19).

This surely is one of the great arguments for the Bible. The Bible faces up to the question, What is man? It tells us where man has come from; it tells us what man is; it tells us what man should be. It accounts for the world as it is. It accounts, yes, for the glorious achievements of man. Christians have no difficulty in accounting for these. They do not have to say that only Christians can be great scientists or great philosophers or great benefactors of society. No, all men are made in the image of God and, by the grace of God, who knows what any man might be able to aspire to in those realms?

So the Christian is able to recognise that there is a greatness of achievement in man; and yet at the same time he is able to see that this image of God is spoiled. It is marred and twisted; it is defiled. The Fall has taken place; man is no longer what he used to be. This evil, this ugliness, this terrible disease of sin has come in and spoiled men, and so you get wars, immoralities, unfaithfulness, child-abuse, and all these other terrible things that we read of in our newspapers day by day. The Bible can account for it: the humanist cannot. According to him, these things should have been eradicated long ago. Mankind should be getting better and better as we stand on the shoulders of each succeeding generation and move up the scale of progress. But this is mere wishful thinking! Man is morally corrupt, and the Bible is able to explain that quite perfectly.

The perfect image
However, this is not all that the Bible has to say about the image of God. What else does it say? It tells us that the problem, this problem of man himself, is incapable of being solved by him. But God is able to deal with it, and God has dealt with it. What God has done is to send into the world his own Son, who is all that man was intended to be in the first place. A number of references in the New Testament to the Lord Jesus Christ speak of him quite specifically and explicitly in this connection:

God, who at sundry times and in divers manners spake in time past unto the fathers by the prophets, hath in these last days spoken unto us by his Son, whom he hath appointed heir of all things, by whom also he made the worlds; who being the brightness of his glory, and the express image of his person, and upholding all things by the word of his power, when he had by himself purged our sins, sat down on the right hand of the Majesty on high (Hebrews 1:1-3).

Christ is 'the express image' of God's person. And Paul, speaking of Christ, says that he is 'the image of the invisible God, the firstborn of every creature' (Colossians 1:15).

You look at Jesus Christ and you see in him the perfect man. Do you recall the words spoken by Pontius Pilate on that fateful night when, humanly speaking, he had the destiny of the Lord Jesus Christ in his hands? He brought Christ out onto the balcony and he said, 'Behold the man!' What he said was true, though he did not really understand it! 'Behold the man!'—the man who is the perfect image of God, the man in whom is no sin, the man who is pure and spotless and undefiled. Jesus is the man who was all that you and I should ever be—the man who is the very image of God. Yes, he is also the Son of God; he is God, God the Son. But humanly he is *the man*, the one who bears the perfect image of God.

The great message of the Bible is that he left heaven and came to earth to deal with this terrible problem—that we, who are made in the image of God, now have that image spoiled and marred. Something needs to be done about it, and Christ is the one who can do it. He did it by living the life that we should live—no sin, no hasty word or impure thoughts, nothing that he ever had cause to regret or call back. A perfect life, and then a sin-atoning death, paying the penalty for our sins. Going up to the cross and bearing our sins in his body on that awful tree. Taking to himself the righteous anger and wrath of a holy God. Dying in the place of sinners and rising again in the very power of God. Rising never to die again—the great resurrection of the Lord Jesus Christ! And now seated in glory on the right hand of God!

This is what the gospel says. However debased or debauched a person may have been in his life, however hopeless, however much of a failure—when that person comes in his sin to the Lord Jesus Christ, something marvellous happens. First, his sins are forgiven; the slate is wiped clean. Not only that, but it is guaranteed to be kept clean in the righteous eyes of God. The sinner is what the Bible calls 'justified by grace through faith' in the sight of God.

God's image restored

That is not all. Something happens not just to the 'standing' of the sinner before God; something happens to the sinner himself. The scriptural phrase for this is that he is 'born again'. He becomes a new creature, raised from death to life. He starts to live for the first time, and a process is begun, a process that will go on moment by moment and day by day throughout his earthly life and will ultimately be brought to perfection when he enters heaven. God restores his image in the sinner. He restores the sinner to what he should be, to all that Adam was, indeed to more than all that Adam ever was! He ultimately restores him to a state of eternal perfection as he bears the image of God. The apostle Paul makes this wonderful truth so clear: 'For whom he did foreknow, he also did predestinate to be conformed *to the image of his Son*, that he might be the firstborn among many brethren' (Romans 8:29).

This is what is happening to the Christian. Sometimes it may not be obvious to us. There are so many vestiges of sin left in us, and we fail and we backslide. But God is at work, and God is fashioning us after the image and likeness of the Lord Jesus Christ, the perfect image of God. Sometimes he does it as he disciplines us, as he chastises us, as he comes and deals with us severely (as we think). Sometimes his discipline is much more gentle and easy to accept. But all the time this is what he is doing: he is restoring that image, bringing us back to what Adam was when first he fell into sin, and indeed beyond what he was, for we shall see Jesus one day and *be like him* (1 John 3:2).

The image is still there, yes, but we know that God is working at it. God is restoring it, making it absolutely perfect. We read the Scriptures, we sit under the preaching of the Word of God. We pray, we think about the Lord Jesus Christ. We meet together with the people of God and have fellowship with them and with God. Through all these means, and more, God is working in us to produce the image that he wants us to demonstrate:

> Now the Lord is that Spirit: and where the Spirit of the Lord is, there is liberty. But we all, with open face beholding as in a glass the glory of the Lord, are changed into the same image from glory to glory, even as by the Spirit of the Lord (2 Corinthians 3:17-18).

That is what God is doing. The technical word that Christians use for this process is 'sanctification'—being made conformable to the likeness of Jesus Christ.

> Changed from glory into glory,
> Till in heaven we take our place,
> Till we cast our crowns before Thee,
> Lost in wonder, love and praise.
>
> (*Charles Wesley*, 1707–88)

You bear the image of God in you, whoever you are and whatever you are. I tell you something else: it is a spoiled image, a marred image; you are not what you should be. Sin has come in, with its devastating consequences. But is the work of restoration taking place? Have you been born again? Do you know anything at all about this ministry of the Holy Spirit as you behold the face of the Lord Jesus Christ, as you read of him and meditate on him and pray to him? Do you know anything about being changed 'from glory to glory, even as by the Spirit of the Lord'?

Or are you like the mass of people in the world who are without God, without hope? Men are not animals; they are human beings, God's special creation. And yet, unless they come to the Lord Jesus Christ, they are destined for doom and destruction in hell. Christ offers himself to you now and tells you that if you come to him, trusting in him and believing upon him, this great work of the re-creation of the image of God in you will commence, only to be completed when you see him face to face.

Chapter Six
The God of the covenant

And God said, This is the token of the
covenant which I make between me and you
and every living creature that is with you, for
perpetual generations: I do set my bow in the cloud,
and it shall be for a token of a covenant between
me and the earth. And it shall come to pass, when I
bring a cloud over the earth, that the bow shall be
seen in the cloud: and I will remember my covenant,
which is between me and you and every living creature
of all flesh; and the waters shall no more become a
flood to destroy all flesh. And the bow shall be in the
cloud; and I will look upon it, that I may remember
the everlasting covenant between God and every
living creature of all flesh that is upon the earth.
And God said unto Noah, This is the token of the
covenant, which I have established between
me and all flesh that is upon the earth.
(Genesis 9:12-17)

The words recorded for us here in Genesis describe some of the events that took place almost immediately after the great and climactic event of the Flood. The Flood is now over, and here is God beginning things again. There is but one family—Noah, his wife, his three sons and their wives—one family that again is going to repopulate the whole of the earth. That there still exists this remnant is evidence of the fact that God is a faithful God; a God who keeps his word; a God who, when he threatens, performs that which he threatens he will do; and a God who, when he promises, fulfils those promises. Through his servant Noah, that 'preacher of righteousness', he had been warning a corrupt, violent and unbelieving world to flee from the forthcoming wrath of God. They would not listen, and God kept his threat.

When the Flood was over, God began to speak not words of judgment, but words of blessing. At the end of the previous chapter we have these words:

And Noah builded an altar unto the LORD; and took of every clean beast, and of every clean fowl, and offered burnt offerings on the altar. And the LORD smelled a sweet savour; and the LORD said in his heart, I will not again curse the ground any more for man's sake; for the imagination of man's heart is evil from his youth; neither will I again smite any more every thing living, as I have done. While the earth remaineth, seedtime and harvest, and cold and heat, and summer and winter, and day and night shall not cease (Genesis 8:20-22).

The promise of God! You and I are witnesses to the fact that God has kept his promise. Seedtime and harvest, cold and heat, summer and winter, day and night have endured and will endure—until that destined time comes when God winds up this world, with all its imperfection and its sin, and ushers in the eternal state. So God is a God who is faithful.

This God comes to Noah and Noah's family and begins to speak to Noah. He makes a promise to Noah that he will establish a covenant with him.

And I, behold, I establish my covenant with you, and with your seed after you; and with every living creature that is with you, of the fowl, of the cattle, and of every beast of the earth with you; from all that go out of the ark, to every beast of the earth. And I will establish my covenant with you; neither shall all flesh be cut off any more by the waters of a flood; neither shall there any more be a flood to destroy the earth (Genesis 9:9-11).

God's initiative

Let me draw your attention to something about God that is exceedingly important. It is clearly demonstrated here, and it can be substantiated from many other parts of Scripture. It is this: God is the God who takes the initiative. God is the God who does not wait for men to come to him. If that were the case he would wait for eternity, and still they would not come. God is the God who approaches sinners, who takes the initiative with them; he comes to them, seeks them out, finds them and brings them to himself.

This happened right back in the Garden of Eden, after that first sin had brought down the judgment of God not only upon Adam and Eve but also upon the whole human race. You remember what happens. God comes down. God seeks out Adam. Adam, in his guilt and foolishness, is hiding away from God, thinking that he will be able to conceal himself from the gaze of God. But God seeks him out. God takes the initiative.

We see the same principle here again. Noah and his family have come down from the ark. The earth is dry once more. The animals are released from the ark and the family begins to try and pick up the threads of their new existence. What happens? God comes. God begins to speak. God enters into this great covenant with Noah. God is the God who graciously takes the initiative with sinners. Thank God for that, because if it were not for that fact, there would be no hope for any of us here! Our God is the God who takes the initiative. This is repeatedly shown to us in both Old and New Testaments.

You find this demonstrated abundantly in the ministry of our Lord Jesus Christ. On one occasion our Lord spoke to his disciples and told them something which is really the same as the truth I am dealing with here. He said: 'Ye have not chosen me, but I have chosen you' (John 15:16). It is always like that; the initiative is with the Lord Jesus Christ. God comes and God seeks. God finds sinners and draws them to himself. 'No man can come to me, except the Father which hath sent me draw him' (John 6:44). Those of us who are Christians are not Christians because one day the fancy came into our minds that we would become Christians. What happened to us was this: God sought us; God put his hand upon us; God drew us to himself.

Exactly the same thing must be true of you if you are to become a Christian. It will not be by your own efforts. It will not be by your seeking somehow to climb up to heaven that you will find acceptance with God. It will be by God coming to you, God seeking you, God inviting you, God showing what is sometimes called 'prevenient grace'— grace that comes before you ever sought him—God looking for you and God finding you. This is one of the great principles of the Bible.

It is not very difficult to understand why it has to be like this. It is true of us, you see, not only before we become Christians, but it is also true of us when we are Christians. Some Christians may feel that they are particularly blessed and gifted by God. I would simply like to remind you of a question that the apostle Paul asks in his first letter to the

Corinthian Church: 'For who maketh thee to differ from another? and what hast thou that thou didst not receive?' (1 Corinthians 4:7). It is not from you. It is from God. All is of grace. God is the God who goes before and who seeks out sinners.

The human predicament

Again, it will not be difficult to show you both why and how this must be. Man is a sinner; you are a sinner; I am a sinner. Every human being that has been born into this world (with the solitary exception of the Lord Jesus Christ) is a sinner. That means, to quote the language of Scripture, that the sinner is at enmity with God. He is resentful in his heart towards God. He does not want God to rule over him. Therefore, if God were to wait for the sinner to come to him, because of the basic inherent corruption that lies at the very heart of a man's being the sinner would never come. In the heart of man there is this alienation, this enmity of the sinner towards God.

Not only that, for the Bible speaks of the sinner in other ways. Sometimes it speaks of the sinner being crippled. He needs to come, but he is unable to do so. There is a remarkable incident in John's Gospel that illustrates this. Our Lord Jesus Christ comes to the pool of Siloam in the city of Jerusalem. Apparently there was a tradition or belief that at a certain time an angel went down and troubled the waters of the pool, and the first man that could get in after the disturbance of the water, whatever his illness, would be cured. When our Lord comes to this pool, he finds a great crowd of men there—poor, sick, crippled men, many of them blind, lame, withered and impotent—waiting for the moving of the water. 'And a certain man was there, which had an infirmity thirty and eight years. When Jesus saw him lie, and knew that he had been now a long time in that case, he saith unto him, Wilt thou be made whole?' The man's answer demonstrates the human predicament: 'The impotent man answered him, Sir, I have no man, when the water is troubled, to put me into the pool: but while I am coming, another steppeth down before me' (John 5:5-7).

You see, this man is really typical, his condition symptomatic, you might say, of the whole human race. There is a cure available, but he has no power to get to the cure. That is the heart of the problem. He is a cripple—and that is what the sinner is, crippled and unable to come to God. He may not recognise it; he probably does not. In fact he may deny it; he may even be angry if it is suggested to him; but that does not alter the matter. He is a poor cripple of a sinner. He needs to come, but he cannot come. His very sin keeps him there in that state of helplessness.

The Scriptures tell us more about the condition of the sinner. Not only is he alienated from God, at enmity in his heart towards God and, like some poor cripple, unable to move himself towards God, but he is also blind—he does not see his condition. You might argue that this shows the depth of the tragedy: he will not recognise the truth about himself and therefore he cannot see his need. He lingers there, but he does not cry to God because he does not see that he has any need of God. He does not see that he needs to have his sins washed away. He justifies himself by pointing to others who he thinks are more needy than he is! He languishes in this state of spiritual blindness, in hopelessness, separated from God. Were God not to come to him in that condition, he would go to hell.

This great principle in Scripture is a necessary principle if we are to have any hope. God is the God who takes the initiative. Here in Genesis 9 this divine initiative is encapsulated in a word that occurs in the Bible for the first time at this point. It is the word 'covenant'. This is a word that occurs many times subsequently in Scripture. God said to Noah: 'And I, behold, I establish my covenant with you, and with your seed after you' (Genesis 9:9). God then gives the details of the covenant, and he speaks of the token of the covenant:

> And God said, This is the token of the covenant which I make between me and you and every living creature that is with you, for perpetual generations . . . And I will remember my covenant, which is between me and you and every living creature of all flesh; and the waters shall no more become a flood to destroy all flesh. And the bow shall be in the cloud; and I will look upon it, that I may remember the everlasting covenant between God and every living creature of all flesh that is upon the earth (verses 12, 15-16).

A covenant God

We are introduced here to one of the great keywords of the Bible. Our God is a covenant God, a covenant-keeping God. A covenant is a type of promise; it is the word you might use if you wanted to make something more than a promise. Promises are often broken, but a covenant is something that you *cannot* break, something that you *will not* break! That is why this word is used—it speaks of the faithfulness of God. Here is something solemn and binding. God pledges himself in this way. He is not offering an opinion or making a suggestion; God is binding himself.

In our society we have some understanding of this word 'covenant', for it is in frequent use as a legal term. Some people, for example, enter into a covenant with the trustees of a particular church or charity to give a certain sum of money. They cannot enter into a covenant lightly and then decide a few days later that they are not going to keep it! There is something solemn, something binding about it. There may be other areas where you have entered into a covenant. Thinking of the end of your life, you may make a will, a last will and *testament*. That word 'testament' really means 'covenant'. A person who feels unjustly dealt by in a will cannot turn round and say, 'I do not like that will! So, let us change the terms of it so that I can get all the money instead of my brother!' No, a covenant has been made, and a covenant must be adhered to.

Here God is entering into a covenant. When Christians partake of the Lord's Supper these words of our Lord are often read: 'This cup is the new testament in my blood, which is shed for you' (Luke 22:20). That is the Authorised Version translation, but most recent versions prefer to say: 'This cup is the new *covenant* in my blood'. Here is God again making a promise, God renewing the promise, God reminding us that the promise has been ratified by the blood of his Son. This is something that God has done—the God who takes the initiative, the God who enters into this unbreakable covenant with his people. Our God is a covenant-keeping God.

More than that, this covenant is a covenant of *grace*. God could enter into a covenant of judgment—and he will do that. Remember the many, many incidents in the course of the Old and New Testaments where men and women who scorned and ignored him discovered that they could not do it with impunity. Sooner or later this covenant-keeping God comes upon them in judgment. Yes, but this is not a covenant of judgment. It is the very opposite; it is a covenant of grace. It begins to speak to us of the grace and mercy of God even though, as God says, the world is so sinful. In the eighth chapter of Genesis we read these very striking words:

> And the LORD smelled a sweet savour; and the LORD said in his heart, I will not again curse the ground any more for man's sake; for the imagination of man's heart is evil from his youth; neither will I again smite any more every thing living, as I have done (Genesis 8:21).

God comes with this covenant of grace despite the sinfulness of men. He enters into a solemn and binding promise that he is not going to send the judgment of a Flood upon the world again.

The sign of the covenant
Then he does something very remarkable. He speaks to Noah and tells him that the sign of the covenant will be the rainbow:

> And God said, This is the token of the covenant which I make between me and you and every living creature that is with you, for perpetual generations: I do set my bow in the cloud, and it shall be for a token of a covenant between me and the earth (Genesis 9:12-13).

The rainbow! Have you ever thought of a rainbow like that? We all know what rainbows are. Sometimes we see a rainbow and call someone's attention to it—'There's the rainbow!' Or perhaps at times you try and remember the order of the colours in the rainbow. A rainbow is a very beautiful thing, isn't it? I once drove from Newport to Abergavenny on a summer evening. I was going to hear a great man of

God preaching. I do not know how you would explain it, but it was as if, in the fields on the right-hand side of the road all the way from Newport to Abergavenny, the end of the rainbow came down and touched the earth! It was one of the most beautiful experiences that I have ever known. Seeing that rainbow seemed to crown the whole occasion.

Now there are two possible ways of understanding the significance of the rainbow as the appointed sign of the covenant, though I am not sure that anybody is qualified to say unequivocally which is correct. Either could be true. In the sermons on the earlier chapters of Genesis, I called your attention to the fact that when God set man in the Garden of Eden there had been no rain. 'The LORD God had not caused it to rain upon the earth, and there was not a man to till the ground. But there went up a mist from the earth, and watered the whole face of the ground' (Genesis 2:5-6). The suggestion has been made that up to the time of the Flood there was a canopy of water vapour encircling the whole earth. Underneath this canopy the climate may well have been humid and equable, with no extremes of heat and cold, and there would not have been the sort of atmospheric conditions needed to produce the effect of a rainbow. But with the coming of the Flood, partly due to the deluge of waters from the heavens, everything was changed. There were new atmospheric conditions, and for the first time a rainbow appeared. God says: 'This is the token of the covenant'. This could well be the explanation as to why God at this point declared that the rainbow was to be the sign of his covenant with Noah. I suggest this as a possibility; I do not think we can say categorically whether or not it is the case.

The other possibility is that the rainbow had been observed as a natural phenomenon from the creation down to the time of Noah. There was nothing new about it; it was something very well-known to the human race. But suddenly God says, 'This now has an added importance. It is a rainbow, as you well know, but I am investing it with a new significance, so that in future whenever you see a rainbow there will be a lesson that you can draw from it. The rainbow will be a reminder to you—as, in a way of speaking, it will function as a reminder to me—that never again will I come in the judgment of a flood upon the earth. Seedtime, harvest, cold, heat, summer, winter, will all take place to the end of the earth.' It was not that God needed reminding, but he is condescending to our weakness and speaking in human terms so that we can say something about God.

This is not far removed from what happens at the Lord's Supper. We use ordinary bread and ordinary wine. There is nothing special about them; but they have a special significance in the communion service. 'This cup is the new testament [covenant] in my blood, which is shed for you' (Luke 22:20). The bread is a token of Christ's broken body. The wine is a token of his outpoured blood. If we accidentally drop the bread on the floor we do not suddenly become panic-stricken and think, 'Oh dear! the body of Christ has fallen to the ground and it might be contaminated!' No, it is ordinary bread, ordinary wine; but Christ has taken these things and it is as if he has said, 'There is a new significance when you do it this way. There is a new significance about these common, familiar, everyday things.'

So too with the rainbow. God may have taken this familiar sign, the beautiful sign of a rainbow, saying: 'You thought of that just as a rainbow in the sky, which you admired when you saw it. But in future I want you, whenever you look at it, to remember that I regard it as a token— a token of this covenant that I have entered into. It will be a token that never again am I going to send a flood of judgment upon the earth until the very end of time. Then there will not be a flood, but the consuming fire of my wrath. But, until that time, seedtime, harvest, cold, heat, summer, winter, day and night will continue.'

There is something remarkable about this, as the Hebrew language has no word for rainbow. It only has a word for the bow, which at the time was used with arrows in warfare. What God is saying is: 'I am going to set my bow, my war bow, there in the clouds. The storm clouds may appear to you to be threatening the judgment of another flood. But it is not threatening judgment; the bow will be a token between you and me. When I see the bow, I will remember—and instead of judgment, I will show mercy to you.' It is as if God took the very instrument of threat in warfare and set it there in the sky, making it a token of his grace and mercy—a pledge that never again will this particular judgment fall upon men.

Have you ever thought of a rainbow like that? Next time you are out after a storm and the sun comes out and you see a beautiful rainbow, do not just say, 'How beautiful!' Ask yourself about the theological significance of it. Remind yourself that, in a manner of speaking, that rainbow reminds God of the unbreakable covenant promise that he made. A phenomenon that could have been a sign of damnation has become instead a token of blessing.

The cross

This is a principle that runs through Scripture and that comes to its great climax in the cross of Calvary. Can you think of anything more repugnant than the cross? The idea of the cross to the Jews was 'Cursed is every one that hangeth on a tree' (Galatians 3:13; cf. Deuteronomy 21:23).

To suggest that the One who was claimed to have come from God should end up being executed on a cross! To the Jew it was a stumbling block and to the Greek it was foolishness They thought it utterly ridiculous.

There is nothing beautiful about the cross. You might argue that one of the lies of Christian history is the way in which many have taken the cross, stark and ugly as it is, and turned it into a thing of artistic beauty, finely moulded and beautiful in its proportions. But it was not like that. The cross was something repugnant and repulsive. It was something that spoke of judgment, an instrument of death, a gibbet that clearly announced that its victim was someone who deserved death and the judgment that fell upon him. What does God do? He takes that very instrument of death and turns it into life. He takes that which was dark and gloomy and causes it to shine with all the brightness of the rainbow. He causes us, when we look at the cross, to see not the story of judgment (although it is there) but the promise of mercy!

Because of this, wherever they went, those first Christians preached Jesus Christ and him crucified. 'Crucified?' said the Greeks, 'Ridiculous! You claim that he is the Messiah, One who has come from God and who can lead you to heaven. And you tell us that he ended up on that instrument of execution, being put to death in that public and most degrading manner?' The Christian says yes—'For the preaching of the cross is to them that perish foolishness; but unto us which are saved it is the power of God' (1 Corinthians 1:18). That which is ugly becomes spiritually beautiful. The instrument of death becomes the means of life. God, the covenant-keeping, merciful God who seeks out sinners, comes and takes what you might have thought was the final token of damnation and judgment, and he makes it nothing less than the very door of entrance into the kingdom of heaven!

That is why, from the New Testament onwards, the Christian message has so clearly been simply this: Jesus Christ was crucified in the place of sinners, and for any sinner that looks to him there is mercy, there is forgiveness, there is peace. When God sees the cross, he sees it as the means whereby sinners like you and me can be reconciled to him. What happened on the cross was nothing less than the sins of vile sinners, such as we are, being taken and laid upon the Lord Jesus Christ and punished in him. The judgment fell upon him, and by his stripes we are healed. That is the message of the gospel—God is seeking you out.

If you are one of those people who think that you can come to God whenever the fancy takes you, let me tell you on the authority of God that you are making a terrible mistake. God has to take the initiative. Thank God he did that in the cross. 'For God so loved the world, that he gave his only begotten Son, that whosoever believeth in him should not perish, but have everlasting life' (John 3:16). I ask you, What do you do with Jesus Christ and him crucified? Do you snap your fingers at God and tell him that he might as well have kept him in heaven? Dare you do that? Dare you look the Son of God in the face and treat him like that? Do you not see in the message of the cross the full token and the final proof that God has loved you? God seeks you. God calls you to believe on the Lord Jesus Christ, sinner though you are—that is the only qualification for coming to Jesus. Come as you are, and find a welcome there in the cross that you might say is the fulfilment of this glorious rainbow—a token of the mercy of God. He is the God who will judge; but ere he judges, he offers mercy to repentant sinners. Come to Jesus Christ and live!

Chapter Seven
God rules on high

And the LORD *said, Behold, the people*
is one, and they have all one language; and
this they begin to do: and now nothing will be
restrained from them, which they have imagined to
do. Go to, let us go down, and there confound their
language, that they may not understand one another's
speech. So the LORD *scattered them abroad from*
thence upon the face of all the earth: and they left off
to build the city. Therefore is the name of it called
Babel; because the LORD *did there confound the*
language of all the earth: and from thence did
the LORD *scatter them abroad upon*
the face of all the earth.
(Genesis 11:6-9)

We have been looking at these important, but much neglected, early chapters of Genesis. My reason for considering them is simple. They contain the foundation message on which the rest of the Bible is built. If you ignore these chapters, then you cannot really understand the rest of Scripture. Yet it is strange how people who neglect these opening chapters of the Bible will turn to certain selected passages, in either the Old or the New Testament, and wonder why they do not understand them. They then presume to dismiss the Bible and its authority. Yet, when you come to the Bible in the way in which it is presented here, beginning, as you ought to, at the beginning, you have a story

117

that is coherent. It is a story that enables you to make sense of the unfolding account, as God goes on to explain to us his dealings with men and women down through the centuries.

I am well aware that many people do not bother with these chapters because they say in effect, 'These things I cannot believe! The Sermon on the Mount, now, I can accept that. Perhaps various aspects of the epistles of Paul as well, and certainly some of the Psalms and the Gospels, I will take those!' But when they come to what they would describe as these 'really primitive' parts of the Word of God—the story of the Fall, Adam and Eve, the Flood, etc.— they go on to say that an intelligent person living at the tail-end of the twentieth century cannot be expected to believe that these things actually happened as they are said to have done.

But I make no apology for saying that I do expect you to believe that these events actually and literally happened. I do this because the Lord Jesus himself placed his stamp on the whole of the Old Testament. You remember that in the Sermon on the Mount, so beloved by many who do not understand it, he said: 'Think not that I am come to destroy the law, or the prophets [terms referring to the Old Testament]: I am not come to destroy, but to fulfil. For verily I say unto you, Till heaven and earth pass, one jot or one tittle shall in no wise pass from the law, till all be fulfilled' (Matthew 5:17-18). At the moment when our Lord spoke those words, the New Testament was not in existence and only the Old Testament was available to him; but he did not hesitate to regard it as the Word of God. He quoted with approval from what many today would regard as the most objectionable parts of the Old Testament, such as the accounts of the Flood and the destruction of Sodom and

Gomorrah. When asked questions about marriage and divorce, he went right back to the end of the second chapter of Genesis, and he quoted from it in order to settle the point at issue.

The incarnate Son of God, the One whose wisdom is infinite, clearly believed that these events happened. Who are we to enter into a controversy with the Lord Jesus Christ and say that we do not believe what he said? Such would be the height of arrogance. So I make no apology for preaching on these chapters, and in particular for coming to the eleventh chapter with its description of events connected with the attempted construction of the tower of Babel. It comes a little while after the account of the Flood, and the covenant that God entered into with Noah after the Flood. The intervening tenth chapter contains a long genealogy, linked to the emergence of various nations, and leads on to what we are considering now.

The chapter opens by telling us that although by that time mankind had spread extensively over the earth, they spoke only one language. 'And the whole earth was of one language, and of one speech' (Genesis 11:1). They had no difficulty in communicating with each other. Usually in our congregation there is quite a range of nationalities. Were we to speak to one another in the smattering of French or German or some other language that we learned long ago at school, we would not get very far, because we would discover that our knowledge has become exceedingly rusty. If you have travelled abroad, you will know full well the difficulty of living among people who do not speak your own language. You may think that they ought to, but they don't—you happen to be in their country, and so much the worse for you! Yet here was a time when there was no such thing as a foreign language. Men, wherever they were, could communicate with one another.

Noah's ark came down upon Mount Ararat, in what today is the north-east of Turkey, just to the north of Mesopotamia. The movement of the people afterwards is described here in Genesis 11: 'And it came to pass, as they journeyed from the east, that they found a plain in the land of Shinar; and they dwelt there' (Genesis 11:2). The plain of Shinar lies between two rivers, the Tigris and the Euphrates, and apparently it was there that they settled.

Man's scheme

Then they began to scheme with one another. 'And they said one to another, Go to, let us make brick, and burn them throughly. And they had brick for stone, and slime had they for morter' (Genesis 11:3). In other words, they were no longer building in the way that they had done formerly (presumably with stonework and masonry), but now they began to manufacture bricks. They burnt them in some sort of kiln to make them more durable. The Authorised Version says: 'And they had brick for stone, and slime had they for morter.' A more modern version would translate 'slime' as 'tar' or 'bitumen'. We all know the Middle East, the Gulf, as the land of oil. In places it lies on the surface. So bitumen was readily available to them, and they used it as mortar or cement for joining bricks together.

So here is the story of what you might call a developing civilisation. The people come and begin to build: 'And they said, Go to, let us build us a city and a tower, whose top may reach unto heaven; and let us make us a name, lest we be scattered abroad upon the face of the whole earth' (Genesis 11:4). It is at this point that you begin to sit up and take notice. Here we have the beginnings of a rebellion against God, but not just on the individual level. Here was a community, a society, a civilisation, conspiring together in an act of rebellion against God.

God had given a clear instruction to our earliest forefather Adam, and he had repeated it at various times. The instruction was that the human race, the descendants of Adam, should multiply and fill the whole earth. Here you see that those descendants—humanity such as it was at that time—liked the situation in which they found themselves. This nice, pleasant, alluvial plain was easy to cultivate; it was an attractive place in which to live; so why should they be on the move? 'Why go any farther?' they must have asked themselves. 'Why venture out into the unknown? We have acquired these skills; we are able to make bricks; we are able to make buildings the like of which our fathers would never have imagined possible. Let us build a city; and in this city let us have a great tower—a tower that is going to reach up to heaven. If we wander away, we can look back and see this tower, and we will know where to come back to! In any case, we are a remarkable group of people—no civilisation like this has ever existed before. They never had our skills. Let us do something to put our stamp, to leave our mark, upon this world! Let us have a great monument that reaches up to the sky!' And that is what they began to do.

It is interesting how sometimes the archaeologist is able to cast little sidelights upon the Word of God. Various books give you pictures or diagrams illustrating their finds. They tell us that in that particular region there are remains of tower structures that were obviously used for religious purposes, though at a later date. One in particular is outside the ancient city of Babylon—or rather, the site upon which it was built and where its remains are to be found. The archaeologists are able to tell us what it was like and to give us some dimensions. One, which may have been years later than the tower of Babel—a great tower or *ziggurat* as these structures were called—had a base ninety metres square. Let me give you the dimensions of the building in which I preach so that you can see how large that is. It is thirteen metres from wall to wall, and thirteen metres up to the peak of the building, which is therefore as high as it is wide. Now the height of just the base of the *ziggurat* was thirty-three metres—that is approximately two and a half times the height of the church—and on top of the base were a further five storeys, each up to eighteen metres in height! Even with my mathematics I could calculate (and then I checked it with the commentaries!) that we might reasonably expect this tower to have been one hundred metres high, or more than three hundred feet. That is no mean achievement. This particular tower may not have been the tower of Babel, but it gives us some idea of the building skills of some of these ancient people and the scale upon which they conceived their building operations. 'And they said, Go to, let us build us a city and a tower, whose top may reach unto heaven; and let us make us a name, lest we be scattered abroad upon the face of the whole earth' (Genesis 11:4).

That was their plan and intention. Whether they had some superstitious idea that they would actually be able to climb up to heaven, or whether it is just a metaphorical statement—'we will build something that is so magnificent that it reaches as it were up to heaven'—is immaterial. What was wrong was that they were neglecting the mandate that God had given to man, that he was to fill the earth and take possession of it and be lord over it. They just wanted a comfortable existence there in the plain of Shinar, building their buildings with the new skill that they had acquired.

God's intervention

Then we read of God's reaction. 'And the LORD came down to see the city and the tower, which the children of men builded' (Genesis 11:5). God doesn't need to come down, of course—he sees everything—but here Scripture is speaking, as it so often does, in what is known as anthropomorphic language.

> And the LORD came down to see the city and the tower, which the children of men builded. And the LORD said, Behold, the people is one, and they have all one language; and this they begin to do: and now nothing will be restrained from them, which they have imagined to do. Go to, let us go down, and there confound their language, that they may not understand one another's speech. So the LORD scattered them abroad from thence upon the face of all the earth: and they left off to build the city. Therefore is the name of it called Babel; because the LORD did there confound the language of all the earth: and from thence did the LORD scatter them abroad upon the face of all the earth' (Genesis 11:5-9).

The word 'Babel' is actually translated, later in the Old Testament, as 'Babylon'. In Hebrew there is a word that sounds almost the same. It is the word for 'confusion', and you see why this particular name was given. 'Therefore is the name of it called Babel; because the LORD did there confound the language of all the earth: and from thence did the LORD scatter them abroad upon the face of all the earth' (Genesis 11:9). That is why people the entire world over speak different languages. That is also why the whole world is populated today. It is partly an act of mercy on the part of God in intervening to stop this scheme of men, and partly an act of judgment as well. How different would it have been if there had never been a tower of Babel!

The story of Babel has a number of lessons, even strange lessons, to teach us. Does it not really describe to us the history of mankind? Again and again you seem to find a little microcosm, as it were, of the story of humanity compressed into a small segment of Scripture. It is as if, in essence, you can see the same story repeated over and over again, but with slight changes in style and outworking, depending on culture and background. This account of the tower of Babel, and of God's judgment upon it, is really the story of the whole of human history since the Fall—and particularly so as the Scriptures unfold themselves from this point onwards. It is the story of mankind, the story of civilisation. What seems to happen repeatedly is that man gets too big for his boots, and then God has to intervene and remind him that he is just a man, and that all his schemes are subject to the overruling providence and sovereignty of God. God seems to allow man to go so far, and then he intervenes. And down come all man's schemes, all his great imaginations, and he is back where he started.

You can find this illustrated repeatedly in secular history. In fact, history could be written in these terms. Much of the Old Testament is certainly written in this way. One civilisation seems to reach the acme of its power; nothing is too great for it to do. Then another power comes on the scene; another maybe insignificant nation begins to arise. Before long the great empire is in ruins, and this new nation and empire is building something else upon those ruins. On and on goes the story: the Egyptians, the Assyrians, the Babylonians, the Medes, the Persians, the Greeks, the Romans, and right down to the present day to the British

Empire that used to be. It is all part of the same story. Men build these great edifices. They become secure and confident in what they are doing and imagine that nobody has ever done anything like this before: 'We [whoever the 'we' happens to be] are the greatest race that has ever lived, and our achievements surpass those of any previous civilisation.' Man begins to boast and to flaunt himself in the sight of God. And God intervenes. God humbles him. God sees the tower of Babel, and what does he do? He comes to these men and scatters them abroad. He causes them to speak different languages so that they cannot communicate with one another, and their great co-operative venture just collapses in ruins.

Let me tell you the rest of the story about that particular *ziggurat* in Babylon that I mentioned earlier. Should you go to Babylon now—if you are able to get there in view of the hostilities that have ravaged that part of the world in recent years—you would not find an edifice three hundred feet up in the sky; indeed you would hardly find the ruins. You see, it was demolished and rebuilt. By whom? You have heard some of their names in the Old Testament. Esarhaddon was the first to rebuild it. Then there was another war, and down it came once more. Nebuchadnezzar was the next to make the attempt. But along came a great Persian monarch, the Emperor Xerxes, and he demolished it. Alexander the Great wanted to rebuild it, and so he tidied up the whole site and cleared away the rubbish. Then he went off to conquer India and died before he could get round to rebuilding the tower. The archaeologists tell us that if you go to that site now, all that remains of the massive edifice that reached so far into the heavens is a pit at least twice as deep as the tower was once high. It is a very striking example of the judgment of God.

The lesson of history

If that actually was the tower of Babel, you might say that God is hurling it down through the centuries. He is causing subsequent generations, subsequent empires and civilisations to bring almost to non-existence the magnificent structure that a former generation had built, thinking that they would reach heaven in the process. God does this. He will not allow anybody or anything ultimately to challenge him but will eventually smite them down. History is the story of the development of man in his sin, in his rebellion against God. It is the tale of man becoming too big for his boots, and provoking God into doing something to humble him and to cut him down to size, so that he might know that he is just a man.

Here then is this act, this corporate act of rebellion against God. That, you might say, is the distinguishing feature about this account of the tower of Babel. It is not just individual men rebelling against God. That was true of man right back as far as the Fall in the Garden of Eden, and every individual from that time onwards has been an individual rebel against God. But here they are planning, scheming, conspiring together. 'And they said one to another, Go to, let us make brick, and burn them throughly . . . And they said, Go to, let us build us a city and a tower, whose top may reach unto heaven; and let us make us a name . . .' (Genesis 11:3-4). This is something that they are doing together arrogantly against God. 'Who is the Lord?' they seem to say. 'Let us get up there and see if he is there!'

That is the spirit man always shows. Do you remember Yuri Gagarin, the Soviet cosmonaut who went up into space? He came back with the pronouncement that there is no God because he did not see him there—as if he could see the invisible God! The arrogance of man, thinking that he can make these pronouncements about God and that he can challenge God! These people were rebels; they were not ready to submit to God's will; they wanted their own will to prevail. And they were so proud of themselves! Who has built anything like this before? Who was ever *able* to build anything like this before? Who ever had the skills that we have? On they went, therefore, with this great engineering project of building this huge tower, and they were so proud of it!

But, you know, you can go to virtually any of the great cities of Europe and see exactly the same thing. Go to Paris and you will see the Arc de Triomphe. Go to Berlin and you will see the Brandenburg Gate. Go to London and you will see Nelson's Column, commemorating the battle of Trafalgar, the glorious achievement of the British Navy. Go round the rest of our capital city and you will see many other monuments to great achievements of our nation in former days. But you know that they will all come down.

In the city of Rome there is a great arch, a triumphant archway, which I have seen. It is called the Arch of Vespasian. When a Roman general went on some great campaign and won a marvellous extension to the Roman Empire, he would bring all his captives and all his booty back to the city of Rome. And Rome would honour him by allowing him to lead his troops in a magnificent procession through the imperial city. But, before that procession took place, a great triumphal arch would be built. The general would march through the archway at the head of his army, and the assembled Romans would cheer and applaud and praise him.

There on that archway in Rome are carved all the symbols of the nations that they conquered. From these we are able to learn what some of the items in the Temple at the time of the Lord Jesus Christ looked like. The lampstands and other items are engraved or chiselled out on this triumphal archway in Rome. Can you not imagine the pride oozing from that general and his armies as they marched through it, perhaps dragging behind them slaves and captives and all the possessions they had taken? But where are they now? Where is the Roman Empire? All that is left is monumental ruin—another tower of Babel, you might say!

It has been like this throughout history. Men pride themselves and build their edifices, thinking that they are great and will leave their mark on history. Then God takes them away. Sometimes he causes these very edifices to decay and to become ruins, so that what was intended as a monument to the achievements of man becomes instead a witness to the foolishness and sin of man and the sovereignty of an almighty God. Our God is a sovereign God, and here he exercises his sovereignty as he deals with the arrogant presumption of these people against his person. He always does it; you cannot challenge him and win. You cannot do it individually; you cannot do it as a nation; you cannot do it as an empire. God is and God will be victorious.

There are many instances of this in the Word of God. The mention of Babylon reminds us of the book of Daniel in the Old Testament. Daniel was one of the Jewish captives carried away by Nebuchadnezzar to Babylon. We read in the fourth chapter of Daniel: 'At the end of twelve months he [Nebuchadnezzar] walked in the palace of the kingdom of Babylon. The king spake, and said, Is not this great Babylon, that I have built for the house of the kingdom by the might of my power, and for the honour of my majesty?' (Daniel 4:29-30). The king is basking in his own glory, looking out over this great city, fully aware of the fact that he is the most powerful man in the world. But:

While the word was in the king's mouth, there fell a voice from heaven, saying, O king Nebuchadnezzar, to thee it is spoken; The kingdom is departed from thee. And they shall drive thee from men, and thy dwelling shall be with the beasts of the field: they shall make thee to eat grass as oxen, and seven times shall pass over thee, until thou know that the most High ruleth in the kingdom of men, and giveth it to whomsoever he will. The same hour was the thing fulfilled upon Nebuchadnezzar: and he was driven from men, and did eat grass as oxen, and his body was wet with the dew of heaven, till his hairs were grown like eagles' feathers, and his nails like birds' claws. And at the end of the days I Nebuchadnezzar lifted up mine eyes unto heaven, and mine understanding returned unto me, and I blessed the most High, and I praised and honoured him that liveth for ever, whose dominion is an everlasting dominion, and his kingdom is from generation to generation: and all the inhabitants of the earth are reputed as nothing: and he doeth according to his will in the army of heaven, and among the inhabitants of the earth: and none can stay his hand, or say unto him, What doest thou? (Daniel 4:31-35).

Would you not think that men would learn their lessons? But they do not. In the very next chapter of the book of Daniel, a descendant of Nebuchadnezzar, a man called Belshazzar, is king. Belshazzar is holding a great feast, an orgy I suppose we would call it, and suddenly a hand appears and starts writing on the wall. Daniel is called upon to interpret what is written:

And this is the writing that was written, MENE, MENE,

TEKEL, UPHARSIN. This is the interpretation of the thing: MENE; God hath numbered thy kingdom, and finished it. TEKEL; Thou art weighed in the balances, and art found wanting. PERES; Thy kingdom is divided, and given to the Medes and Persians. Then commanded Belshazzar, and they clothed Daniel with scarlet, and put a chain of gold about his neck, and made a proclamation concerning him, that he should be the third ruler in the kingdom. In that night was Belshazzar the king of the Chaldeans slain. And Darius the Median took the kingdom, being about threescore and two years old (Daniel 5:25-31).

The princes of this world

It is always the same. The apostle Paul expresses it in perhaps an unusual way when he explains that, when he preaches the gospel, he deliberately scorns the wisdom of the world:

And I, brethren, when I came to you, came not with excellency of speech or of wisdom, declaring unto you the testimony of God. For I determined not to know any thing among you, save Jesus Christ and him crucified. And I was with you in weakness, and in fear, and in much trembling. And my speech and my preaching was not with enticing words of man's wisdom, but in demonstration of the Spirit and of power: that your faith should not stand in the wisdom of men, but in the power of God. Howbeit we speak wisdom among them that are perfect: yet not the wisdom of this world, nor of the princes of this world, that come to nought (1 Corinthians 2:1-6).

It is the same with all the princes of this world—they 'come to nought'! This is the principle of the tower of Babel. Go to some of the great statues in London, equestrian statues or statues of great statesmen. Who are they? You do not know! I could not help reflecting on this some years ago as I watched a newsreel of the unveiling in Queen Street, Cardiff, of a statue of the late Aneurin Bevan. Do you remember who he was? Or have some of you perhaps never heard of the founder of the National Health Service? In the news programme they stopped some passers-by in Queen Street and asked them what they thought of the statue. They said nice things about the statue, but when asked 'Who is it a statue of?' they did not know. 'Who is Aneurin Bevan?' they asked. Who would have thought in the late fifties or sixties that his name would have been forgotten quite so soon? The princes of this world come to nought—even those greater than Aneurin Bevan ever was! They all come to nought.

Some years ago, the then Chancellor of the Exchequer was interviewed in the light of the trouble on the world stock markets. He said something to the effect that no worldwide storm could possibly wreck the British economy. I thought, 'Man, you are a fool!' He may have been making a political statement, but it was not the statement of a man who thinks deeply about the history of the world—or of a man who thinks deeply about God! You see (and I put it like this deliberately), when men arrogantly and presumptuously exalt themselves against him, and pride themselves on their achievements, God delights to come and humble them. He did it here with the tower of Babel. 'And the LORD said, Behold, the people is one, and they have all one language; and this they begin to do: and now nothing will be restrained from them, which they have imagined to do' (Genesis 11:6). God intervenes, and he intervenes in this humbling way that scatters them across the face of the earth.

As I look back over the great empires of the earth I cannot help remembering a poem. It was written at the time of what might be called the zenith of the British Empire.

God of our fathers, known of old,
    Lord of our far-flung battle line
Beneath whose awful hand we hold
    Dominion over palm and pine—
Lord God of Hosts, be with us yet,
Lest we forget—lest we forget!

The tumult and the shouting dies;
    The captains and the kings depart;
Still stands Thine ancient sacrifice,
    An humble and a contrite heart.
Lord God of Hosts, be with us yet,
Lest we forget—lest we forget!

Far called, our navies melt away;
    On dune and headland sinks the fire:
Lo, all our pomp of yesterday
    Is one with Nineveh and Tyre!
Lord God of Hosts, be with us yet,
Lest we forget—lest we forget!

If drunk with sight of power, we loose
    Wild tongues that have not Thee in awe,
Such boastings as the Gentiles use,
    Or lesser breeds without the law—
Lord God of Hosts, be with us yet,
Lest we forget—lest we forget!

For heathen heart that puts her trust
  In reeking tube and iron shard,
All valiant dust that builds on dust,
  And guarding, calls not Thee to guard,
Lord God of Hosts, be with us yet,
Lest we forget—lest we forget!

There is something almost prophetic about this poem that Rudyard Kipling wrote in 1897, when the British Empire was at the height of its power:

  Lord God of Hosts, be with us yet,
  Lest we forget—lest we forget!

All our might, all our power, becomes 'one with Nineveh and Tyre!' And you can add to that, Rome, Greece, Babylon, Babel. God casts down everything that exalts itself against him. This comes to a conclusion almost at the end of the Bible, in the book of Revelation. Here Babylon, this developed civilisation that it was to become, is conceived of as the enemy of God exalting itself against God:

And he cried mightily with a strong voice, saying, Babylon the great is fallen, is fallen, and is become the habitation of devils, and the hold of every foul spirit, and a cage of every unclean and hateful bird. For all nations have drunk of the wine of the wrath of her fornication, and the kings of the earth have committed fornication with her, and the merchants of the earth are waxed rich through the abundance of her delicacies. And I heard another voice from heaven, saying, Come out of her, my people, that ye be not partakers of her sins, and that ye receive not of her plagues. For her sins have reached unto heaven, and God hath remembered her iniquities (Revelation 18:2-5).

'Babylon the great is fallen'—and so falls everything that exalts itself against God. It happens individually; it will happen to you. You may think that all is well with you, that even God—if, as some of you might say, there is a God—even God cannot touch you. He can do it, he is able to do it, he is committed to doing it and he will do it! God cannot allow you to exalt yourself against him. All your hopes are going to be dashed. You hope for health; it will fail you one day. Your wealth, such as it is, you will have to leave behind you. You may depend on popularity and affability, but friends are so fickle. All can go, and all will go. In the future, when your name is mentioned, people will say, 'Who was he? Who was she?' A nonentity, forgotten even by those who should remember you.

A lasting kingdom

The tower of Babel! God intervening, God judging, God humbling. There is only one thing that lasts—the kingdom of God, the city of God. We read of it in the twelfth chapter of the epistle to the Hebrews, when the writer speaks of the great confidence that the child of God has in the Lord Jesus Christ. He speaks of the urgency of listening to and heeding the God who speaks to us from heaven:

See that ye refuse not him that speaketh. For if they escaped not who refused him that spake on earth, much more shall not we escape, if we turn away from him that speaketh from heaven: whose voice then shook the earth: but now he hath promised, saying, Yet once more I shake not the earth only, but also heaven. And this word, Yet once more, signifieth the removing of those things that are shaken, as of things that are made, that those things which cannot be shaken may remain. Wherefore we receiving a kingdom which cannot be moved, let us have grace, whereby we may serve God acceptably with reverence and godly fear: for our God is a consuming fire (Hebrews 12:25-29).

He is a God who will allow no rivals, the God who is pledged to intervene and humble anything that exalts itself against him and his knowledge.

Is that what you are doing? What is your life being built on; what are your foundations? Are you in some puny little way erecting a tower of Babel that you think is impregnable and indestructible? God will cast it down, God will intervene. There is only one place where you will be secure, only one foundation on which you can build. There is only one kingdom, one empire, that will never fade away, and that is the kingdom of our God and of his Son, the Lord Jesus Christ. You enter that kingdom not by virtue of your efforts, your works or your potential, but by the grace of God. You enter as your sins are washed away in the blood of the Lord Jesus Christ shed upon the cross for sinners.

I tell you in his name that, despite what the world says about you and whatever it ultimately makes of you, if you call upon him you will be in that kingdom. You will receive a kingdom that cannot be moved; you will have that confidence that you have listened to the God whose Word is never a lie and whose promises are never broken; the God who has promised never to leave you nor forsake you. He is the God who has promised one day to take you to heaven, the God who has pledged one day to set you there on the very thrones of heaven praising and glorifying him.

I ask you, Is your kingdom like the tower of Babel, like some modern Babylon, sooner or later destined for ruins? Or are you in the kingdom of God, building on this sure and firm foundation? Repent while there is time and opportunity. Come, before God has to intervene and destroy all that is most precious to you.

Chapter Eight
The Lord of history

And I will bless them that bless thee,
and curse him that curseth thee: and in thee shall
all families of the earth be blessed.
(Genesis 12:3)

These words constitute the most comprehensive promise to be found anywhere in the Bible. They come in a section in which we are told of the call of God to Abram to leave Ur of the Chaldees and venture out in faith in the living God. And they are preceded by a chapter that is largely composed of a genealogy.

I wonder what you do when in your regular Bible reading you come to such a passage? Do you jump over the genealogy to the next verses that are easier to read? You may be tempted to say, 'Why on earth is something like this in the Word of God? The names are hard to pronounce. We are told how old they were when they had their first child, how long they lived after that, the number of children they had, and what happened to the next one! What has such a passage to do with me?' you ask. 'I can understand why a verse like John 3:16 and many other passages which are filled with blessing are in the Scriptures, but why did God bother to put these genealogies in?' I will tell you why it was. God bothered to put them in because he wanted us to be absolutely sure that we are dealing here with something that really happened.

The ancient Jews have the advantage over us here. If anybody asked you this evening who your father was, you would be able to tell him. If you were asked about your grandfather and when and where he was born, you might be rather vague. But if it were your great-grandfather's details that were the subject of the enquiry, you might wish you had never been asked! Yet not only the Hebrews, but also many people in different parts of the world today, could recount to us with meticulous exactness their ancestry for generations and generations. They could do this because such things matter to them. They want to know where they come from. They want to have their roots firmly planted in history.

The Bible is a book of history. It is not a book of fantasy, nor is it a book of moral stories, telling us how to live but with their moralising having no roots in history. Right from the beginning, and right on to the end, the Bible is a book about history. It deals with real things and real persons. It deals with the world in which they lived and in which we live. Ultimately it tells us that there is going to be a new heaven and a new earth in which dwell righteousness. Existence and all that is concrete is not somehow going to cease and be no more. The eternal state will be a real state, just as our present condition is, and that of our ancestors was, a real condition. These genealogies are here because God is serious about history; it is as if he is telling us that he is the Lord of history. They witness to the fact that God was to choose a people with a real, developing line of descent. These lists of people are not myths, sagas or pieces of ancestral folklore. The people they mention really existed; the events they described really happened.

God is making the link, the genealogical link, down through the centuries to Abram. His name is later changed from Abram to Abraham because of the great change that took place in him and the great blessing of God that descended upon him. Until this point in the record, we have been presented with what is, in a sense, general history: the whole history of humanity, the terrible catastrophe of the Flood out of which only one family was rescued, and then, from that family, the rebuilding of the entire human race.

A pivotal figure

Noah had three sons, Shem, Ham and Japheth. In this family tree, attention is drawn to one of his sons, Shem, and his descendants. We are told, 'These are the generations of Shem: Shem was an hundred years old, and begat Arphaxad two years after the flood' (Genesis 11:10). Then the family tree goes on through Arphaxad, Salah and Eber right down to this man Abraham. It is as if God is becoming more specific, more particular, narrowing things down; and from this moment in the Word of God Abraham becomes a pivotal figure.

Abraham is often referred to in the New Testament. Jesus told the story of the beggar Lazarus sitting at the gate of a rich man. Both men died, and Lazarus went to heaven. Looking upward from hell to heaven, the man who in this life had been rich saw Lazarus in 'Abraham's bosom': that is, in a place of safety and security (Luke 16:23).

The Jews prided themselves on having Abraham as their ancestor. On one occasion when arguing with John the Baptist they turned on him and said, 'We have Abraham to our father' (Matthew 3:9). They regarded descent from Abraham as being the one thing that mattered: 'We can trace our ancestry back to Abraham, and that makes us different from the rest of the world!' In one sense it was true, for it did make them different from the rest of the world; but their pride and arrogance were wrong.

God made promises to Abraham, and we shall see some of these later in this chapter. It was in fulfilment of these promises that Christ came and died. Have you ever considered this fact? We are here tonight because of what God said to Abraham in Ur of the Chaldees, two thousand or more years before the birth of the Lord Jesus Christ. Had God not spoken to Abraham we would not be here worshipping him, because Christ would not have come. There would have been no salvation, no gospel, no hope, nothing to cheer us as we move through life to the inevitability of death. But, thank God, he did speak to Abraham. He called him and began to work something out in the history of the world that was to reach its great culmination in the coming of the Lord Jesus Christ.

These genealogies found in the early passages of Scripture tell us that God is the Lord of history. Unlike the so-called gods of other world religions, our God is involved in history. This is not the case with other faiths, the Muslim faith, Hinduism, Buddhism, and so on. None of them has anything that speaks of their god coming down into history, being incarnated as a man in history, as the Lord Jesus Christ was. None of these faiths sees the need for God to come into the world. They do not see the plight of man as being so desperate that nothing but the eternal God leaving heaven and coming down to earth to be born as a baby at a specific place and time will meet that need. The Bible sees the necessity of this because God, the Lord of history, takes history seriously. God, seeing the sin of men and women in history, planned to enter the very creation that he had made, the very history that he in his sovereignty is superintending, in order that that he might rescue sinners.

In these verses there is a significant development in the outworking of the plan of God. 'And I will bless them that bless thee, and curse him that curseth thee: and in thee shall all families of the earth be blessed' (Genesis 12:3). There is something very personal, something very direct, that God begins to do at this point. This man Abraham, what was he? He was a pagan living in Ur of the Chaldees. The archaeologists say that when Abraham lived there, Ur was right down on the Persian Gulf. It is now miles from the sea because of silting up or geological changes. There was a great civilisation in Ur of the Chaldees. Its site has been excavated and evidence found of a great and articulate civilisation.

Abraham was a great man in Ur of the Chaldees, but even though he came from this godly line of Shem he was a pagan. By this time, of course, many generations had passed. You know how it happens: godly fathers have children, then grandchildren, then great-grandchildren—and the farther they get from their origins, the more they seem to decline spiritually. Some of you are living evidence of the fact that godly parents may have an ungodly child, or one with just the form of godliness; and then comes the next generation, and even the form is gone. All that is left is evil, and there seems to be an ongoing story of decline and degeneration. I think we ourselves have been living through years in which that process has been not only proceeding but accelerating in our own land.

That is the sort of thing that must have happened here. Shem, who had come through the Flood, knew full well who the living God was. He cannot have failed to tell his son Arphaxad, born two years after the Flood, the marvellous story of God's deliverance. He would have told him also what a terrible place the world had been when he was young, with its dreadful violence, lust and disorder. He would have recounted how God had spoken to his father Noah and told him that his patience was virtually exhausted. God had said that there would be one hundred and twenty years, and then he would wipe out the human race—with the exception of those who came into the special boat that he had commanded Noah to build. And it happened. One day it started raining and there were terrible convulsions in the earth beneath. This flood of waters rose higher than the highest mountains—and for over a year that state of things prevailed. Eight persons were in the ark with all the animals that God had brought into it. In due time the ark touched down on dry land; they let the animals out of the ark and they came out themselves. Then they started living a normal life all over again.

I wonder how many times Shem told Arphaxad these things? Then Arphaxad tells his son Salah about his grandfather and what happened in his day. But as one generation succeeds another it becomes more remote. Nothing is more typical of the human race than the fact that each succeeding generation thinks it knows better than those who have gone before—that nobody is quite as intelligent as you and I! We all instinctively think that our fathers and grandfathers were not up to our standard. Life may teach us that we are fools to say that, but we seem to go on believing it. There is this deterioration, this degeneration. Succeeding generations become worse and worse.

Doubtless the story of the Flood became mixed up in the minds of later generations. One of the remarkable things that anthropologists tell us is that seemingly unconnected ancient peoples from different parts of the world all have a story of the Flood. These stories do have certain elements in common, but all sorts of weird and magical and even vile incidents appear in the local versions of the story. It is not difficult to understand how that essential truth was added to by succeeding generations that eventually spread over the whole earth. They began to twist and pervert the essential truth and story of the Flood.

Abraham, many years down the line from Seth, does not worship God. He is a pagan living in Ur of the Chaldees. We are told later on in the Old Testament, as Joshua is about to leave the children of Israel:

And Joshua said unto all the people, Thus saith the LORD God of Israel, Your fathers dwelt on the other side of the flood in old time, even Terah, the father of Abraham, and the father of Nachor: and they served other gods. And I took your father Abraham from the other side of the flood, and led him throughout all the land of Canaan, and multiplied his seed, and gave him Isaac (Joshua 24:2-3).

Joshua recognises the truth that Abraham was a pagan, who worshipped idols when he lived in Ur of the Chaldees. From what we read of him subsequently in the Word of God, we can also say that he was a rich, powerful and highly intelligent man.

God speaks
Then one day God speaks to him. 'Now the LORD had said unto Abram, Get thee out of thy country, and from thy kindred, and from thy father's house, unto a land that I will shew thee' (Genesis 12:1). How would you respond to such words? What if God came to you and told you to pack up everything that you were familiar with, and to emigrate—not in comfort, with all your belongings sent on before you and with a house and job waiting for you there in another

land, but to become a wandering nomad? You would be living in tents for the rest of your life, working your way up through the Middle East to the Fertile Crescent as it is sometimes called, up the basin of the Tigris-Euphrates. You would stay for a time at a place called Haran, and then, when your father Terah dies, move on from Haran and come down to the land God has promised you, this land of Canaan. But you do not actually take possession of it. In fact the only portion of the Promised Land that Abraham could call his own during his lifetime was the little patch of land in which he buried his wife! The land had been promised to him and to his descendants, but he was a wanderer through it for most of his life. That was the call that came to Abraham in Ur of the Chaldees. 'Get thee out of thy country, and from thy kindred, and from thy father's house, unto a land that I will shew thee' (Genesis 12:1).

What an unlikely man for God to speak to, and what an unlikely thing for God to say to such a man! But this is the story of the Bible. God comes to strange people, unlikely people, unpredictable people, and makes demands of them that they find disturbing and unsettling. God speaks to them, and suddenly the whole of their lives, their hopes and aspirations, all they have set their hearts upon, is turned upside down. What God tells them to do is quite different from everything they had planned. That is the story of the Bible. Here you have this man Abraham being spoken to by God and hearing and responding to the call of God. The writer of the epistle to the Hebrews brings home to us forcefully and yet simply what was involved:

By faith Abraham, when he was called to go out into a place which he should after receive for an inheritance, obeyed; and he went out, not knowing whither he went.

By faith he sojourned in the land of promise, as in a strange country, dwelling in tabernacles with Isaac and Jacob, the heirs with him of the same promise: for he looked for a city which hath foundations, whose builder and maker is God (Hebrews 11:8-10).

God spoke to Abraham in this disturbing way. What amazing things were going to happen to him, and what a life-story he would have! God had promised him: 'And in thee shall all families of the earth be blessed' (Genesis 12:3). Later on God promises him a seed: 'And [God] brought him forth abroad, and said, Look now toward heaven, and tell the stars, if thou be able to number them: and he said unto him, So shall thy seed be' (Genesis 15:5). Abraham was an old man when God first promised that he would have a son by Sarah his wife. Humanly speaking it was impossible— yet God had promised. Eventually, when Abraham was about ninety-nine years old, Sarah conceived and bore a son, Isaac. You might think that Abraham's troubles were over, but when Isaac was growing up God spoke to Abraham again. God told Abraham to take his son, his only son Isaac, and to offer him up as a sacrifice upon a mountain that God would tell him of. Abraham's faith was being put to the test. God was to deal in a very strange way with this man.

Abraham is mentioned at this point in Genesis because God is about to widen out his promise. It is as if, at this point, the whole of humanity has been narrowed down to this one man Abraham. God has set his saving purposes upon this man, and so the line of Seth comes down to Abraham. Then God speaks to Abraham and tells him that there is to spread out from him a blessing so great that it is hard to describe it adequately. All families, kindreds, nations of the earth are going to be blessed. Abraham then has a son Isaac; Isaac has a son Jacob, and the story of the Old Testament develops. Before many chapters have passed there is not just a family but a nation—the children of Israel. Jacob's other name is Israel, and he has twelve sons, the children of Israel. You have here the beginnings of what was to become the great Jewish nation.

The rest of the Old Testament is taken up with the story of that nation. They go down to Egypt in a strange way, in a time of famine, and end up there as slaves and captives. But God brings them up out of Egypt. There is a mighty deliverance at the Red Sea. Then God brings them through the wilderness and gives them his law on Mount Sinai. He parts the River Jordan before them and puts them in the Promised Land. You may think that their troubles are over, but in a sense they are only beginning, because of the iniquity and deceit of their own hearts. Before very long these people whom God has blessed are falling into the customs and even the worship of the pagan nations around them. God sends judges to deal with them. Next God raises up a king among them called Saul, who proves himself to be an abject failure. Then come great King David and Solomon and the rest of the kings. But what happens? The Israelites refuse to learn from their own history. They turn their backs on God. God sends the ten northern tribes, or Israel as they are called, into a captivity from which they were never to return. Almost a hundred and fifty years or so afterwards, Judah (the remaining two tribes around the city of Jerusalem), refusing to learn from what God has done to Israel, is carried off to captivity in the land of Babylon.

God's promise

In all this God is concerned to preserve a nation. Why?

Because from that nation, the seed of Abraham, is going to come into history the God-man, who will be the Saviour of sinners. So this marvellous history story in the Old Testament of God's dealings with Israel first widens out the blessing, and then narrows it down, to focus on the Lord Jesus Christ. What do we say about the nation of Israel? They were not only oppressed but also corrupt. They did not want the truth. They scorned the Lord Jesus Christ. They put him on the cross and rejoiced when he was crucified. It is as if all Israel narrowed down to this one person, Jesus Christ, and from that focal point of history once more there is a great expansion of blessing.

If you are a Christian, you are one because of this promise to Abraham. 'And in thee shall all families of the earth be blessed' (Genesis 12:3). In the opening chapter of Luke we learn how the angel Gabriel comes to the virgin Mary and announces to her that she is going to give birth to the Messiah. After that, Mary goes to her cousin Elizabeth, the mother-to-be of John the Baptist. The two women rejoice and Mary says: 'He hath holpen his servant Israel, in remembrance of his mercy; as he spake to our fathers, to Abraham, and to his seed for ever' (Luke 1:54-55). A little later on in the same chapter Zacharias, the father of John the Baptist, having been struck dumb in the Temple because he did not believe the message of the angel to him, is given back his speech after his son is named John. We read:

And his father Zacharias was filled with the Holy Ghost, and prophesied, saying, Blessed be the Lord God of Israel; for he hath visited and redeemed his people, and hath raised up an horn of salvation for us in the house of his servant David; as he spake by the mouth of his holy prophets, which have been since the world began: that we should be saved from our enemies, and from the hand of all that hate us; to perform the mercy promised to our fathers, and to remember his holy covenant; the oath which he sware to our father Abraham, that he would grant unto us, that we being delivered out of the hand of our enemies might serve him without fear, in holiness and righteousness before him, all the days of our life (Luke 1:67-75).

Both Zacharias and Mary had understood that Jesus Christ was born as a result of this promise made to Abraham. God had entered into this great covenant. God, the God who never breaks his word, God who is the Lord of history and who allows nothing to frustrate his will and his purpose, eventually sent his Son into the world.

When speaking of the entrance of the Lord Jesus Christ into the world, the apostle Paul said:

But when the fulness of the time was come, God sent forth his Son, made of a woman, made under the law, to redeem them that were under the law, that we might receive the adoption of sons. And because ye are sons, God hath sent forth the Spirit of his Son into your hearts, crying, Abba, Father (Galatians 4:4-6).

Paul is telling us that God, at the precise moment he had planned from all eternity, sent forth his Son. He sent him in fulfilment of this promise. In the previous chapter Paul writes:

Even as Abraham believed God, and it was accounted to him for righteousness. Know ye therefore that they which are of faith, the same are the children of Abraham. And the scripture, foreseeing that God would justify the heathen through faith, preached before the gospel unto Abraham, saying, In thee shall all nations be blessed' (Galatians 3:6-8).

And then a few verses later:

That the blessing of Abraham might come on the Gentiles through Jesus Christ; that we might receive the promise of the Spirit through faith. (Galatians 3:14)

This is why I said that you and I would not be Christians but for the promise God made to Abraham in Ur of the Chaldees—and not the promise only but its great fulfilment in history by God, the sovereign Lord of history.

It is this majestic God that I am trying to set before you now. Foolish men and women sometimes dismiss God. If they deign to mention him at all they represent him as a weak person to be manipulated and twisted by the creatures he has made. How wrong they are! They need to stand back and see him as the sovereign Lord that he is. He is the God who has ordered all history, the God who was there in the Garden of Eden. The God whose holiness and justice were manifested in the judgment of the Flood. The God who entered into a covenant with Noah and the whole of humanity. The God who called Abraham out of Ur of the Chaldees, and gave him the promise of a country and, more than that, the promise that from him would come the One through whom all the nations will be blessed.

Thank God that the promise of God has come upon Gentiles, and not only upon Jews, because of the faith of Abraham. Did you notice that Paul said, 'And the scripture

. . . preached before the gospel unto Abraham, saying, In thee shall all nations be blessed' (Galatians 3:8)? To Abraham, with all his dimness of understanding and misconceptions because of his heathen background, God spoke the gospel when he said, 'And in thee shall all families of the earth be blessed' (Genesis 12:3). God spoke the gospel to Abraham not in the fulness of revelation that we have in the New Testament, but with sufficient clarity nonetheless. God said, 'Abraham, from you is going to come the One who will be Saviour of the world. All nations, all kindreds, all people will be able to turn to him and have salvation.'

Believing God

Abraham believed God. Can you imagine what was said about him in Ur of the Chaldees? 'Have you heard about Abram? Do you know what he is up to? He is selling his business, selling his house, buying tents and some camels, and talking about going up north into the desert and not coming back! He says that God has spoken to him. We do not know what he means when he speaks about God. Haven't we gods enough in our temples? Have you ever heard of anyone doing something as stupid as that? Something must have turned his head! He is not just going on his own; he is taking his family and his old father with him up into the desert!' It must have been difficult for Abraham to live with all that ridicule, but God had spoken and Abraham obeyed.

It is the simple lesson that is re-enacted over and over again in the Scriptures. God speaks; people hear and obey. Has God spoken to you—this sovereign Lord of history, this God who, even at this stage in history, is showing that his heart is full of compassion for poor wretched sinners? In order to bring salvation to them he selects this man

Abraham. Of him God will make a great nation, and from that nation will come the Lord Jesus Christ, as far as his humanity is concerned. This is the purpose of God. 'But when the fulness of the time was come, God sent forth his Son, made of a woman, made under the law, to redeem them that were under the law' (Galatians 4:4,5). He did this so that you and I might enter into the blessing, the promise that God made to Abraham: 'And in thee shall all families of the earth be blessed' (Genesis 12:3).

Do you dismiss God and think that he is not worthy of your consideration? Do you think that you are some sort of intellectual cut above him, so that you do not deign or condescend to stoop down and deal with such trivialities? Shame on you if that is your attitude! This God is the living God. This God sits upon the circle of the earth and is able to look down upon these little grasshoppers, which is all that we are in his sight. Yet he is able and willing to speak to us and to come and bless us.

Have you trusted in him? Have you seen the great purpose of God in the plan of history and the coming of his Son into this world? Have you yielded to him? If not, do it now! Stop dismissing him. Repent of your arrogance and your pride. Humble yourselves under the mighty hand of God and see that he has blessing for you personally. Come to the Lord Jesus Christ, who has come into the world that people like you and me might be saved instead of being lost. Believe upon him and enjoy the great blessing of salvation.

Daniel

Servant of God under four kings

Geoff Thomas

Daniel has a very powerful message for Christians today. For its main theme is that it is possible to resist the values of a hostile society without withdrawing from it. Daniel served God and four kings without compromise and with wisdom and integrity.

Like Daniel, Christians need to unmask and confront the idols of our day, but they will not be able to do so unless they share his burning conviction that God alone is to be worshipped and served. This lively exposition will put much needed resolve into our souls and thus help us stand for God in our day.

Geoff Thomas, minister of Alfred Place Baptist Church, Aberystwyth, since 1965, is well known as a conference speaker on both sides of the Atlantic. He is also a frequent contributor to a number of Christian journals.

151pp. ISBN 1 85049 146 1

Published by
Bryntirion Press
Bryntirion, Bridgend CF31 4DX
Wales, UK

Griffith John
Apostle to Central China

Noel Gibbard

Short of stature, Griffith John is by any reckoning a spiritual giant. Born in 1831 into a humble Welsh-speaking home in Swansea, he lost both is parents early in life to outbreaks of cholera. Overcoming considerable obstacles he became a missionary to central China with the London Missionary Society. The year of his departure was 1855, the length of his service over fifty years, before old age and increasing senility brought about his return to England where he died 26 July 1912.

In China he immersed himself in the language and culture of the country to such an extent that he was able to debate with Confucianist scholars. On his many journeys Griffith John braved hostile crowds. Though he made a noble contribution in the field of education, organised health care and built hospitals, his master passion was to spread the Christian message.

A man of tremendous energy that was sustained by his uncomplicated and powerful faith Griffith John remained faithful to his missionary calling all his days. Yet he experienced depression and knew great sorrow at the loss of wife (twice) and children. Truly this fine biography shows that Griffith John could aptly be called Mr Greatheart.

250pp. ISBN 1 85049 150 X

Published by
Bryntirion Press
Bryntirion, Bridgend CF31 4DX
Wales, UK

Welsh Calvinistic Methodism

A historical sketch of the Presbyterian Church of Wales

William Williams

Introduction and notes by Dr Gwyn Davies with an appendix by D. Martyn Lloyd-Jones on 'William Williams and Welsh Calvinistic Methodism'

Howel Harris, Daniel Rowland, William Williams—Pantycelyn, were all leading figures in a revival movement which became known as Calvinistic Methodism. Blending Calvinism and experimental religion, this 'theology for the heart' (Eifion Evans), through the church which arose from it, gave to Wales a distinctive ethos in which great preaching and deep piety were combined in a dynamic synthesis.

In this very readable book William Williams captures the essence of a profound spiritual awakening which transformed the life of eighteenth and nineteenth century Wales.

William Williams (1817–1900) was a Calvinistic Methodist minister and popular preacher who wrote in both Welsh and English. This is his best-known book. Gwyn Davies lectures in Church History at the Evangelical Theological College of Wales, Bridgend.

319pp. ISBN 1 85049 147 X

Published by

**Bryntirion Press, Bryntirion, Bridgend CF31 4DX
Wales, UK**

Encounters with God

Some Lesser Known Characters
of the New Testament

Peter Williams

In twenty-four readable chapters Peter Williams draws out challenging lessons from stories of characters as different as Festus, the sophisticated pagan; Lydia, the first European convert; and Silas, the man who lived in the shadow of the apostle Paul. These and many others come alive as real flesh and blood people, so very like us in the temptations they knew, the struggles they experienced, and the pressures they faced from living in a pagan society.

Most of the characters are testimonies to the grace of God at work in human weakness, but a few are salutary warnings of the dangers of trifling with the gospel or making shipwreck of the faith.

Read with an open Bible and a prayerful spirit, this book will challenge you to a closer walk with God and spur you to share your faith with others.

140pp. ISBN 1 85049 121 6

Published by
**Bryntirion Press, Bryntirion, Bridgend CF31 4DX
Wales, UK**

Gypsy from the Forest

A new biography of the
international evangelist Gipsy Smith (1860–1947)

David Lazell

In this major new biography of Gipsy Smith, David Lazell brings a remarkable evangelist to life fifty years after his death in 1947. Born in a gypsy caravan in the Epping Forest and without a day's formal education in his life the Gipsy, as he was known, became an internationally renowned evangelist who preached to thousands—in his native Britain, Australia, Canada, New Zealand, South Africa and especially the United States where he was always warmly received.

A pioneer of co-operation in evangelistic campaigns, one of the early religious broadcasters, a fine singer of gospel songs, Gipsy Smith emerges from this book as a warmly human figure whose great passion in life was to make Jesus known to others.

256pp. ISBN 1 85049 132 1

Published by
**Bryntirion Press, Bryntirion, Bridgend CF31 4DX
Wales, UK**

God Spoke to them

Character studies of Old Testament people

Peter Williams

The Old Testament has many memorable characters. Some are notable examples of faith in God. The lives of others warn us against following in their steps. So in this book we meet people as different as Cain who murdered his brother, Daniel a young man who wouldn't be brainwashed, Hannah a godly mother, and Caleb a man of conviction and courage.

From their stories—and those of others—Peter Williams skilfully draws out spiritual lessons for today.

223pp. ISBN 1 85049 139 9

Published by
Bryntirion Press
Bryntirion, Bridgend CF31 4DX
Wales, UK